D1314597

PECULIARITIES
OF THE
PRESIDENTS

PECULIARITIES

OF THE

PRESIDENTS

STRANGE AND INTIMATE
FACTS NOT FOUND
IN HISTORY

BY

DON SMITH

4584

Printed by
WILKINSON PRINTING COMPANY
Van Wert, Ohio

Drawings by
EDWARD McCANDLISH
Van Wert, Ohio

DEDICATION

PREFACE

The author spent nine years in studying the peculiarities of the presidents. He traveled many thousands of miles in visiting their homes, talking with their relatives, and in interviewing authorities on their lives.

Many musty volumes have given up their forgotten treasures. Countless letters have been written to verify the strange and unique facts related in this book.

The author has endeavored to bring out the human side of the presidents. Some of them were rich, some were poor, some were men of outstanding ability, others were only mediocre, yet the stories of their lives are most interesting.

September, 1938

SECOND EDITION

The enthusiastic reception of this book by educators, and the general reading public, has been most gratifying. It has necessitated the early printing of this second edition.

If you have any rare clippings or information regarding the Presidents, the author will be pleased indeed to hear from you.

DON SMITH

Van Wert, Ohio
June, 1939

QUESTIONS
Can You Answer Them?

EDUCATION

MARRIAGES

INAUGURALS

PHYSICAL

WHITE HOUSE

ACTIVITIES

ODDITIES

RETIREMENT

FINANCE

DEATHS

CHRONOLOGICAL TABLE
Showing Years of Service

Presidents		1	2	3	4	5	6	7	8
Washington	1789-1797								
John Adams	1797-1801								
Jefferson	1801-1809								
Madison	1809-1817								
Monroe	1817-1825								
John Q. Adams	1825-1829								
Jackson	1829-1837								
Van Buren	1837-1841								
W. H. Harrison	1841	Served 1 month							
Tyler	1841-1845								
Polk	1845-1849								
Taylor	1849-1850	Served ⅓ term							
Fillmore	1850-1853								
Pierce	1853-1857								
Buchanan	1857-1861								
Lincoln	1861-1865	Served 4 yrs. 1 mo.							
Johnson	1865-1869								
Grant	1869-1877								
Hayes	1877-1881								
Garfield	1881	Served ½ year							
Arthur	1881-1885								
Cleveland	1885-1889								
Benj. Harrison	1889-1893								
Cleveland	1893-1897								
McKinley	1897-1901	Served 4 yrs. 5 mos.							
Theo. Roosevelt	1901-1909								
Taft	1909-1913								
Wilson	1913-1921								
Harding	1921-1923	Served 2 yrs. 5 mo.							
Coolidge	1923-1929								
Hoover	1929-1933								
F. D. Roosevelt	1933								

Six Presidents died while in office

KEY TO ILLUSTRATIONS

EDUCATION

What President Was Taught to Write by His Wife?

Johnson was a tailor and never pretended to be anything but a tailor. As a small boy he was apprenticed to the trade and was thus deprived of all opportunities of education.

But his marriage, to a very talented woman, opened for him a new life. She first taught him to write, and then broadened his outlook by constantly reading to him while he sat on his tailor's table, making suits of clothes.

Johnson, an East Tennessean, was ardent in his support of the Union cause. In 1864, as a result of this loyalty, combined with the fact that he came from a dominantly Confederate state, he was nominated and elected vice-president and at Lincoln's death became president.

What President Made His Own Edition of the Bible?

Acquaintances of *Jefferson* considered him an unbeliever, for he never discussed religious matters, thinking them each person's own problem. However, when he died, his own copy of the Bible was found among his possessions. After he had taken the sayings of Jesus from Matthew, Mark, Luke and John, he pasted them in a blank book.

This valuable book, prepared by Jefferson's own hand, is now on exhibition in the National Museum in Washington.

What Two Presidents Were Shorthand Experts?

Madison wrote the minutes of the Constitutional Convention in his own system of shorthand. These notes he laboriously transcribed at night. They were the only official record of the actual proceedings of this great convention, and hence of the utmost value. After Madison's death, in 1836, these intimate notes were sold to the Government, by Mrs. Madison, at a price sufficient to keep her for several years.

Wilson was the other shorthand expert, writing all of his speeches first in shorthand, and then, typing them himself.

What President Never Saw a Map of the United States Until He Was Nineteen?

Fillmore was self-made and self-educated. At the age of fifteen, his knowledge of books was limited to the Bible and a hymnal, and at nineteen he had never seen either Shakespeare's works or a map of his own country. As a young man he was a clothier's apprentice, living in western New York, then the frontier.

He became acquainted with a young school teacher, Miss Abigail Powers, whom he later married. They were both interested in books, and together they mapped a four-year course of study, which enabled him to teach school, and, at the same time, follow his trade.

Mrs. Fillmore's intense liking for books continued, so it is not surprising that the first White House library was installed in 1850, by President Fillmore. Mrs. Fillmore had very poor health, but endeavored to be present at all White House functions, being greatly aided in entertaining by her young daughter, recently graduated from college. Mrs. Fillmore suf-

What President Never Voted Until He Was Sixty-two?

(See page 10.)

fered under the strain of public life but attended the
inaugural services of President Pierce, and remained
to welcome Mrs. Pierce to the mansion. In doing
so she caught cold and died three weeks later at the
Willard Hotel.

An Honor Student

Taft was the only American to serve his country,
both as the President of the United States, and as
Chief Justice of the Supreme Court. Either was a
great honor. He was a splendid student, and at Yale
was second in scholarship in a class of 120.

Andrew Jackson had a very rudimentary education. The only book of fiction he ever read during
his lifetime was the "Vicar of Wakefield."

Twenty-four of the 31 presidents were lawyers,
yet only two had experience as judges. They were
Taft and Jackson.

Twenty-one of the thirty-one presidents were college men. However, two never finished their college
courses.

What President Never Voted Until He Was 62 Years Old?

Taylor had served in many military campaigns in
distant and unsettled parts of the country. Thus it
is not surprising that he never voted. Furthermore,
he never bothered himself about politics, and took
no interest in national affairs.

Immediately following the Mexican War the
Whigs were searching for a candidate for president.
They desired a popular personage, perhaps a general, whose name at the head of the ticket would
insure victory at the polls.

So in 1848 *Taylor* was asked by the Whigs if he
would be willing to run for president, and, after de-

liberation, he stated that he might be willing to do
so. Then they asked him if he was a Whig or a
Democrat, and to this he replied that he did not
know, as he had never voted. Regardless of such
lukewarm interest the Whigs asked him to run and
elected him in spite of the fact that he was supported by no definite platform. Taylor died after
serving only one-third of his term.

What President Often Read Three Books an Evening?

Theodore Roosevelt had unusual ability as a reader.
He could glance at a page and in the time it would
take the average person to read a sentence, would
finish it entirely. He wrote nearly 3000 articles for
publication, and more than 150,000 letters in seven
and a half years in office.

"Teddy" did everything intensely and expected
others to apply themselves with similar vigor.
To see others, with spare time, irked him and led him
to exact unnecessary demands. For example, he gave
an official order that each of the army officers should
ride on horseback 30 miles per day for three consecu-
tive days. To show that this could be done he himself rode 106 miles in a single day.

Roosevelt was the best known hunter of all the
presidents, and after retirement went on a big game
hunt in Africa. He also hunted in South America,
where he was stung by an insect, which gave him
a fever from which he never fully recovered.

College Presidents.

But two college presidents became presidents of
the United States. They were Garfield and Wilson.

William and Mary College gave us three presidents: Jefferson, Monroe and Tyler. West Point
gave us but one—U. S. Grant.

What President Was a Tailor and Was Taught to Write by His Wife?

(See page 10.)

Harvard has given us the first and the last (1938) college-trained presidents—John Adams and Franklin D. Roosevelt. John Q. Adams and Theodore Roosevelt also graduated from Harvard.

What President Made 140 Speeches in 30 Days and Never Repeated a Single Address?

Benjamin Harrison occupied the White House between the first and second terms of Grover Cleveland. He was a president of outstanding ability and a marvelous scholar, but he had a cold personality, and did not gain the enthusiasm of the people whom he met personally. Perhaps it was his heavy beard which concealed any possible smile. Harrison could charm vast audiences with his oratory, but if he later met his hearers individually, one by one, in his office, each would turn away—his enemy.

However, he accomplished one feat that no other American president has ever equalled. He made an official tour to the Pacific coast, and during his 30-day trip made 140 addresses, and never repeated a single address. It is true that some were set speeches, carefully prepared in advance, but most were given on a few minutes' notice, before various types of audiences, yet none were repetitions. Chauncey M. DePew said, in his autobiography, that Harrison had the finest legal mind of any president who ever sat in the White House. After his retirement, he earned as much as $150,000 a year as a practicing attorney, in Indianapolis. He was retained by the Government in an important case.

What President Had a Vocabulary of 62,000 Words?

Wilson was one of our best educated presidents and had a working vocabularly of 62,000 words. He did not start to school until he was nine. He resembled Jefferson in mental habits.

Wilson was the greatest platform speaker of his generation, an educator, historian, politician, statesman and international leader. He had great powers of concentration.

His activities were of the widest range. He had a strong will, confidence in himself, lots of courage, and was a man of charming manners. He loved to fight for a good cause. He was elected after only two years of political life.

Wilson played golf both summer and winter. When snow was on the ground, the balls were painted black. He rarely kept score, playing purely for sport. He was occasionally on the golf course as early as five o'clock in the morning.

Upon his first night in the White House, when Wilson was ready to retire at 11:00 o'clock he discovered that the trunk containing his personal belongings was still at the depot.

Wilson was a life-long Presbyterian, the son of a Presbyterian minister, yet he lies buried in the Episcopal Cathedral in Washington.

Mrs. Wilson had all of her husband's letters copyrighted. None can be printed without her permission.

Neither Wilson's private secretary, Tumulty, nor his former adviser, Colonel House, was invited to attend the funeral of Wilson.

MARRIAGES

What President Married the Same Wife Twice?

Jackson's wife Rachel had previously married Louis Robards whom she left because of his cruelties. Unable to force her return Robards brought suit for divorce in a Virginia court, taking pains to make public the action. After the proper expiration of time Jackson married her. However, two years later Robards made it known by another suit, in a Kentucky court, that he was still married. This caused Jackson great mental agony and after Robards had completed his divorce suit, Jackson had a second marriage ceremony with Rachel.

He was extremely sensitive regarding this second marriage and his enemies taunted him much about it. For 37 years he kept two loaded pistols in readiness to avenge his wife's honor.

Mrs. Jackson was short, stout, unattractive and uneducated, but her devotion to him knew no bounds. While the General was in the army she carefully managed his slaves, plantation and money matters. She was an ardent Presbyterian and gave liberally to the church. Both black cigars and corn-cob pipes were common in that day, so her use of them was not so strange.

Mrs. Jackson never lived in the White House for she died between the time of her husband's election and his inauguration. She was arrayed for burial in the same white satin dress which she had planned to wear in the inaugural ceremony.

Sons of Preachers

Four of our presidents were reared in parsonages. They were—Arthur, Cleveland, Wilson and Hoover.

What Bachelor President of 49 Married a Girl of 22?

Cleveland was the only president to be married in the White House. However, both Tyler and Wilson were married during their presidencies, the former in New York City, and the latter in Washington, at the home of his bride.

Cleveland had a very happy marriage. The ceremony was held in the Blue Room, with a few close friends present. At its conclusion, and still hoping to avoid publicity, the bridal couple departed for their train by way of the back gate. But they were pursued by an army of reporters, who followed them to the Maryland mountains, where they had anticipated a quiet honeymoon.

What President's Wife Smoked a Corn-Cob Pipe in the White House?

Taylor's wife was a pioneer woman, far better acquainted with frontier hardships than with the social life of Washington.

General Taylor had served in the regular army for 40 years, and for most of that time his wife had been with him. She had lived with him in tents, army barracks, and among the Indians.

Mrs. Taylor never wanted her husband to become president, saying that it would deprive her of his company. She went reluctantly from their plantation in Louisiana to the White House and never took part in any public functions. She enjoyed smoking a corn-cob pipe in the privacy of her own room.

Which President?

His predecessor in the presidency was also his
    successor.
Made 140 speeches in 30 days, yet never re-
    peated a single address.
Earned $150,000 a year practicing law, after
    retirement.
Our coldest President.

(See page 10.)

What President, Who Entered the White House 97 Years Ago, Has a Living Grandson Only Ten Years Old? (1938).

Tyler became president in 1841, upon the death of William Henry Harrison. His first wife was an invalid and died in the White House soon after her arrival there.

A year later, Tyler, then 54, married a girl of 20. To them was born Lyon Tyler who was later to become an outstanding historian and educator, and finally president of William and Mary College for a period of twenty-nine years. At 72, Lyon married a young woman of 32 and to them were born two sons, one in 1925 and another in 1928. Thus these boys of today are direct grandsons of President Tyler, who entered the White House 97 years ago.

What President's Wife Caused the Planting of the Cherry Trees in Washington?

Mrs. Taft was a great lover of nature, well traveled, and a careful student of the flowers and trees of each country visited. Her own garden was beautiful in spring and summer. When she visited Japan, as the wife of the Secretary of War, the cherry trees were in full bloom. Admiring them greatly, she resolved to obtain some for Washington.

In 1907 Mrs. Taft had 80 cherry trees imported and planted along the Potomac. Her interest so impressed a famous Japanese chemist, Dr. Jokichi Takamino, who was then living in this country, that he arranged for a shipment of 2000 similar trees as a gift from the City of Tokyo to the City of Washington. However, on arrival, the trees were found to be infested with insects, necessitating their destruction.

Two years were then spent in preparing another shipment, this time of 3000 trees. Upon arrival in the fall of 1911 this shipment passed inspection and was accepted by Mrs. Taft in the name of the Government. Professional landscapers artfully arranged the trees in groups of odd and even numbers, which, in Japan, signifies a message of welcome.

Each year, during the first week of April, these trees blossom, tinting the waterfront of Potomac Park with a beautiful radiance. The thousands of visitors who come each season little realize that this once mosquito infested swamp owes much of its present beauty to the planning and interest of Mrs. Taft.

What President of 54 Married a Girl of 20?

President Tyler's first wife died early in his administration. He had become acquainted with Miss Julia Gardner, the daughter of a friend who was killed in an accident while a member of a presidential cruise. Their marriage was a very happy one, despite the fact that there was a difference of 34 years in their ages, and he had grown children older than his new wife.

Many people, after serving in public office, find it embarrassing to obtain work and gain a livelihood. Such was the case with Tyler. He served as a road boss and even kept the "village pound" for stray cows and horses.

Tyler lived on an estate east of Richmond, on the way to Williamsburg, in what was then the longest house in Virginia. The structure extended for about 400 feet, section after section being added.

During the Civil War McClellan's soldiers marched past. Recalling that Tyler was a former President of the United States, but was now a member of the Confederate Congress, the soldiers in course of the campaign entered the beautiful estate. Destructive marks can still be seen in the rooms, where even the furniture has been but little changed during the last 75 years.

Tyler had 14 children, seven by his first wife and seven by his second.

What President Was Overcome by Grief at a White House Wedding?

Nellie Grant as a little girl held her father's hand while he delivered his first inaugural address. In so doing she won the hearts of the citizens of Washington and thereafter remained an object of their interest.

After completing her formal education the president's daughter traveled in Europe. On her return voyage she became acquainted with Algernon Sartoris, an Englishman of a dignified and wealthy family. Shortly thereafter, they announced their wedding for May 21, 1874. President Grant and his wife opposed the marriage from the first, but finally gave their consent despite the fact that they did not wish their daughter to marry a foreigner.

The ceremony was elaborate with the Marine Band furnishing the music. The bride's lace-trimmed gown cost $2000 and the wedding gifts from 200 guests were valued at $60,000. Menus for the banquet were printed on white satin, and each guest upon leaving received a piece of the wedding cake. Beautiful flowers were brought from Florida for the large East Room and their fragrance added greatly to the charm of the event.

At the wedding Grant did not attempt to conceal his great sorrow. After Nellie Grant and her husband had left the White House on their wedding trip, the President was missed. He was discovered in his daughter's room, sobbing, with his head buried in her pillow. Later, the Grants and their daughter were reconciled and after retiring from the White House they visited the young couple in England.

What Recent President Was Married by a Catholic Priest Although Both He and His Bride Were Protestants?

Hoover and Lou Henry became acquainted while they were both students at Leland Stanford University. After graduation he went to the Orient, as a mining engineer, and she returned to Monterey, California, where she taught in the public schools.

Friendship ripened, through correspondence, and when Hoover was twenty-five they became engaged to be married. Hoover was a Quaker, his fiancee an Episcopalian, but Monterey had no Protestant pastor to perform the ceremony.

Father Ramon Mestres was the local Catholic priest, and an old friend of Lou Henry, as a girl. The priest was also justice of the peace, and through a special permission of the bishop, he was allowed to marry the young couple.

After the wedding ceremony, they took a train for San Francisco, and that very day sailed for China.

What President Sent a Special Message to Congress that His Son Had Been Insulted?

John, the son of *John Quincy Adams*, was very bitter against Russel Jarvis, the editor of a Washington newspaper. Jarvis, accompanied by his wife, attended a White House reception, and was publicly insulted by young Adams. Jarvis waited until the President's son came to deliver a message to Congress from his father and in the corridor of the Capitol Jarvis slapped the young man's face. This greatly hurt the Adams pride. The President wrote a special message to Congress about the insult and a congressional investigation was held, but no report was ever filed.

What President's Wife Was Known as "Lemonade Lucy"?

Mrs. Hayes was the first college graduate to be mistress of the White House, and was considered the most popular one since the days of Dolly Madison. She and her husband did not use liquor in any form, and after due consideration decided not to serve any wines during their stay at the White House. This caused great consternation among the citizens of Washington, and many feared international complications. Cartoons were drawn enlarging upon the situation and dubbing Mrs. Hayes as "Lemonade Lucy."

Great pressure was brought upon President and Mrs. Hayes, urging them to serve wine. Even the cabinet members and their wives offered advice. Both the President and his wife were entreated to serve wines "for the honor of the country."

At one reception, an orange drink was served, which tasted exactly like rum. In fact, many of the guests thought it was rum. Weeks afterwards it became known that a flavoring had been discovered which gave the concoction the taste of rum, and it took an expert to detect the difference.

Mrs. Hayes loved to live in the White House. She liked to explore the attics, store-rooms, and basement. She soon arranged all the treasures and relics of past administrations, so that they could be enjoyed by others in the future.

She greatly enjoyed flowers, and each day arranged from twelve to fifty bouquets for friends, hospitals and institutions. She was very charitable. On one Christmas she distributed forty turkeys, with complete dinners, at her own expense, to needy families. She taught her children to save their pocket money and to buy gifts for less fortunate

Which President?

At 54 married a girl of 20.
Borrowed money to attend his own inaugural.
Was burned in effigy on White House lawn.
Entered White House 97 years ago, yet, has
   living grandson only ten years old (1938).

(See page 10.)

children. She left Washington greatly loved by the poor and admired by the church people.

Many circulated the report that Hayes, through stinginess, had saved most of his salary. However, the President, in retirement, made it known that he returned home from Washington with less than $1000 in savings.

Mrs. Grant's Appearance

Mrs. Grant had a peculiar squint eye. While in the White House she suggested that an operation be performed upon it for correction. However, Grant objected, saying he had always known her that way.

What President's Wife Saved the Life of Madame LaFayette?

During *Monroe's* ministry to France, at the close of the eighteenth century, a bloody reign of terror broke out in Paris. Many loyalists were imprisoned including Madame LaFayette, who was condemned to die.

Mrs. Monroe was a very timid woman, but her husband had been an officer under LaFayette in the Revolutionary War and they were ready to do everything in their power to save this wonderful friend of America.

Mrs. Monroe called at the prison, being presented as the wife of the American diplomat. She asked to see Madame LaFayette, who was later brought from her cell. The meeting was touching, as both women bowed in grief. It so affected the French authorities that the next day Madame LaFayette was given her freedom. She joined her husband in an Austrian dungeon. Later both visited America and were guests at the White House while Monroe was president.

What Two Presidents Celebrated Their Silver Wedding Anniversaries in the White House?

On New Year's Eve, 1877, President and Mrs. Hayes celebrated their silver wedding anniversary in a very happy manner. Mrs. Hayes wore her wedding gown and was attended by the President's niece, who at the age of eight had first attended them. The Marine Band played Mendelssohn's Wedding March and the couple stood before Bishop McCabe who had married them a quarter of a century before, and who again gave the blessing. The guests were life-long friends, many of whom had come from Ohio.

The unique part of the ceremony was the christening of a six-weeks-old niece, a sister of Mrs. Taft. Although the guests were requested not to bring presents, one came from the President's former army regiment. It was a silver plate in ebony frame, and was inscribed "To the Mother of the Regiment."

In June of 1911, President and Mrs. William Howard Taft followed precedent by having a silver wedding anniversary celebration.

What President's Daughter Eloped with Jefferson Davis?

Taylor's younger daughter eloped with Jefferson Davis. Her father was greatly angered and declared he would not touch the young man with a "pair of tongs." Even the daughter's early death did not bring them together, and their estrangement continued for many years. However, during the Mexican War, Jefferson Davis became a lieutenant under General Taylor. The West Point graduate showed such splendid bravery on the battlefield, that they embraced, and old "Rough and Ready" became reconciled.

What President's Wife Never Liked to Live in the White House?

Mrs. Pierce was a very backward and retiring woman, disliked public life, and did not want her husband to become a candidate for the presidency. Some years before his nomination Pierce had resigned from the United States Senate and returned to his New Hampshire home, because his wife did not like to live in Washington, and plainly said so.

Pierce's young son, Benjamin, evidently inherited his mother's dislike for public life, as he told a boy friend that he hoped his father would not be elected president because they did not like to live in Washington. However, in spite of his father's success, the boy never had to live in the White House, for he was killed in a train wreck near Boston, a month after his father's election.

Who Was Our Only Bachelor President?

Buchanan, the predecessor of Lincoln, never married and was our only bachelor president. When a young man he had had a happy love affair and was engaged to be married, but the couple were estranged by outside influences. A short time later the girl died, perhaps by suicide. The future president begged permission to view the remains and accompany the relatives to the grave, but his letter was returned by the angry father, unopened.

Forty-four years elapsed, and Buchanan died. Among his private papers, in the vault, was a package of old love letters with a note *"Please do not open these."* His wishes were respected and they were burned without the seal being broken.

For twenty years Buchanan was an unsuccessful candidate for the presidency, although he had held many important diplomatic posts. At last, when he

Which President Is This?

His wife saved life of Madame La Fayette.
Carried Revolutionary bullet in his shoulder.
First President to occupy present White
   House.
Died on 4th of July.

(See page 10.)

received the unexpected honor, he said, "Years ago, I wanted to reward my friends and punish my enemies. But now, after all these years, the friends I hoped to reward have passed away, and the enemies I intended to punish have long since become my friends."

Although a bachelor, his life in the White House was very happy in a social way, with Harriet Lane, his niece, as a most popular hostess. Miss Lane commemorated her uncle's loyalty by bequeathing $100,-000 for a monument in Washington to his memory. Buchanan was the only president to be elected from Pennsylvania. His old home, Wheatland, near Lancaster, is now an historical shrine.

A Diplomatic First Lady

Mrs. John Q. Adams was once besieged by a delegation of ladies from Virginia to influence her husband in a certain military appointment. She heard them courteously and then replied: "Truly, ladies, though Mesdames Maintenon and Pompadour are said to have controlled the military appointments of their times, I do not think such matters appertain to women; but if they did, and I had any influence with Mr. Adams, it should be given to Mrs. Scott, with whom I became acquainted while traveling last summer."

Wife and Secretary

James K. Polk was the only Speaker of the House to become President. Mrs. Polk was the only president's wife to act as her husband's private secretary. Polk died less than four months after his retirement. He was survived by his wife for 46 years.

Three of the first four presidents married widows. They were: Washington, Jefferson and Madison.

John Adams and *John Q. Adams* were the only presidents to be married over 50 years. They are the only two presidents to be buried side by side.

Theodore Roosevelt and *John Q. Adams* were each married in London.

Theodore Roosevelt gave the bride away when *Franklin D. Roosevelt* was married. (Franklin D. married his distant cousin, a favorite niece of Theodore.)

Mrs. Harding was for ten years manager of her husband's newspaper, as well as a contributing writer. While he was in the White House, President Harding sold his newspaper, *The Marion Star*, for $480,000.

A Clever First Lady

Mrs. Theodore Roosevelt wanted to avoid the ordeal of shaking hands with a large crowd of persons, so instead of wearing a corsage at the first public reception, she carried in her hand a large bouquet of flowers. Naturally, no one would think of asking her to lay down the flowers to shake hands, and thus she avoided the trying ordeal.

An Adoring Husband

Chester A. Arthur's wife died one year before he became president. By his own orders her room in New York was left untouched for many years.

INAUGURALS

At What Inaugural Ball Were Tickets Sold for $20.00 Each?

Grant's second inaugural was held on March 4th, 1873. Very elaborate preparations were made, since his former ball had been a keen disappointment, due to insufficient space and poor management.

This time a temporary structure was erected at an expense of $60,000. The main ballroom was 300 feet long and 150 feet wide, and at one end a stage was prepared for the president and his party.

Decorations consisting of flags, bunting and evergreens and several hundred singing canaries were provided, for an extra welcome. As it was before the days of electric lights, some 2500 gas jets had been installed in various parts of the immense hall and reflectors carefully arranged behind them for additional illumination.

The event had been advertised for months, both in the city of Washington and throughout the country. Tickets were greatly in demand at $20.00 each. But with all the elaborateness of the preparation for dancing and banqueting, there was no arrangement for bitter cold weather and the heating facilities were far from adequate.

The presidential party arrived on scheduled time, but did not remove their wraps, and soon departed for a warmer atmosphere. The birds were there, but failed to chirp. It was pitiful to see them tuck their heads under their wings in a vain effort to keep warm. Many died before morning.

The champagne and ice cream were frozen solid and were quickly passed up by the guests in favor of something hot. The entire party left long before

midnight, and the event was in many respects as
disappointing as the ball four years before.

What Was the Coldest Inaugural Day in History?

The day of *Grant's* second inauguration, March
4th, 1873, was the coldest inaugural day in history.
There was a fierce wind and the thermometer regis-
tered four degrees above zero.

Flags and decorations were torn away, the breath
of the musicians condensed in the valves of their
instruments, and many of the marchers fell exhausted from the cold. The ambulances were kept
busy. High prices had been paid for the stands, but
the heavily bundled visitors quickly deserted them.

The President delivered his address in spite of the
bitter cold, and the return to the White House was
made with all possible speed.

What President Was Secretly Sworn into Office?

President Hayes was kept in suspense for four
months as to the outcome of the election of 1876.
This was perhaps the bitterest campaign in history.
It was heated, exciting and close.

March 4th, 1877, fell on a Sunday. Grant was the
outgoing president and his term expired then. If
Hayes were to be sworn in on Monday, March 5th,
the country would be without a president for one
day.

Grant was worried. He gave an evening farewell
dinner party on Saturday, March 3rd, to which
Hayes and his wife were invited. Before the guests
arrived for supper, Chief Justice Wait, and a small
group, assembled in the Red Room where Hayes was
quietly sworn into office. Announcement was not

Who Is This?

"Old Man Eloquent."
Had his clothes stolen while swimming in the Potomac River.
Only President to die in the capitol.
Left a diary of twelve volumes.
Saw battle of Bunker Hill, yet lived to serve in Congress with Lincoln.

(See page 10.)

made to the guests at the dinner party, or to anyone else, until Monday, March 5th.

In spite of the uncertainty as to who would be the new president, at least 30,000 visitors were in Washington to witness the inauguration. President Hayes was greeted enthusiastically.

The entire route of the parade was beautifully decorated. Ten thousand torch bearers marched up Pennsylvania Avenue, singing campaign songs. They crowded into the White House grounds and called for President Hayes. The waving of torches and exploding of fireworks on the lawn made a very imposing scene. There was no inaugural ball, but a reception was held at the Willard Hotel.

Historic Chair

Grant used the same chair for his inaugural which had formerly been used by Washington at the first inauguration in 1789. The owner, who lived in New York, loaned it for this occasion.

Coolidge and *Arthur* were each sworn into office at two o'clock in the morning.

Washington and *Harding* used the same Bible in taking the oath of office at their inaugurations.

Cleveland was the first president to deliver his inaugural address without notes. All previous presidents read their manuscripts.

A Thoughtful President

Cleveland had a great love for children and requested that the children of the Convent of the Sacred Heart, at Albany, be given a holiday on his inauguration day. In spite of all his other duties, he did not forget the matter, but sent a check of $50.00 to provide a celebration.

Grover Moves In

Among the many memorable features of the Cleveland parade at his first inauguration, was the arrival of the President's baggage. A crowd waiting patiently in the covered stand across from the White House found lots of entertainment in watching an open wagon piled high with shabby and scarred trunks, marked "G. C.", which turned in at the White House gates. The crowd sent up shouts of "Grover is moving in."

When Were Hundreds of Hats and Coats Lost at an Inaugural Ball?

Grant's first inaugural ball, March 4th, 1869, was held in the Treasury Building. The evening was bitter cold, the space inadequate and the event grossly mismanaged.

Guests who ventured to the ball found crowded conditions and no adequate place to check their wraps. Many could not get near the door of the banquet room, let alone be seated at tables. They had banquet tickets but could not use them. Many ladies became separated from their escorts and sat on the floor, cold and hungry.

What Was the Most Hilarious Inauguration?

Jackson, of Tennessee, was considered the first western president. His predecessors had been men of polished manners, and, with the exception of Washington, all were college men. John Quincy Adams, his immediate predecessor, moved out of the White House on March 3, and refused to ride with Jackson in the inaugural parade.

Pennsylvania Avenue was lined at an early hour with Jackson's pioneer friends, many of whom had traveled, by horseback, for several hundred miles over the mountains to see "Old Hickory" inaugurated. Upon the return of the parade to the White House the noisy crowd clamored for refreshments, and soon drained the barrels of punch which had been prepared.

In their excitement the new President was pushed aside, and his aristocratic political opponents watched in disgust as the roughly dressed backwoodsmen, with their coon-skin caps and muddy boots, climbed on the upholstered furniture, for a glimpse of their hero. A great deal of china and glassware was broken, and the East Room was filled with a noisy mob.

What Inaugural Parade Was Made Through Ten Inches of Snow?

An unusually heavy snow storm gripped Washington on the day of *Taft's* inauguration. Ten inches of snow had fallen during the sixteen hours immediately preceding the parade, preventing many of the intended paraders and visitors from reaching the city.

Six thousand workmen finally cleared the snow from the inaugural route, and the parade started. The thirty thousand marchers and one hundred bands were cheered by the watchers, despite the fact that they themselves were half frozen from standing in the bitter wind.

What President Lost His Inaugural Address?

Lincoln had prepared his first inaugural address at his Springfield, Illinois, home. It had been put into type by his friend, the local printer, and the four copies locked up in a "grip-sack" which was given to his oldest son, Robert, for safe-keeping.

Upon arrival at Harrisburg, Pennsylvania, Lincoln asked his son where the message was. Robert was much embarrassed, and said that he believed, in the confusion, he had allowed a waiter to take the grip. Upon further inquiry at the hotel, the president decided that if the waiter had taken it, it would be found in the baggage room. Hastening there he found an immense pile of baggage and a grip which looked familiar. The key fitted perfectly but the contents, a flask of whiskey and some collars were not his. Tumbling the baggage right and left, Lincoln continued the search until he found the all-important document.

What President Shook Hands with 6576 People in Five Hours?

Genuine sincerity in meeting people, regardless of their political status, characterized *President* and *Mrs. Harding*. This attitude was in distinct contrast with that of the last few years of the preceding administration, when the White House was isolated during the severe illness of President Wilson.

One of the first official acts of Harding was to have the gates opened and admit the public to the interior of the White House, which Mrs. Harding had brightened by means of flowers placed in the long darkened corners. Thereafter, a stop at the mansion and meeting the president became an expected event for the Washington visitor. At their first New Year's reception, in 1922, the Hardings shook hands with 6576 people in five hours. During the ordeal Mrs. Harding found that her right hand became so swollen that it was necessary to use her left, and that her gloves became so discolored that she changed them several times. During their brief occupancy of the White House it is estimated that the Hardings greeted 400 to 3000 people a day.

Guess Who

Most unhappy President.
Lost in woods on way to Washington.
Died on 4th of July.
Refused to ride with successor in inaugural
  parade.
Only President who previously served two
  terms as Vice-President.

(See page 10.)

Moving the Capitol

Most people think that each of our presidents took office on March 4th, and in the District of Columbia. Washington, however, was not inaugurated until April 30th. He was sworn into office in New York City, on Wall Street, where the Treasury Building now stands. John Adams, his successor, was inaugurated in Philadelphia. Thomas Jefferson was the first president to take office in Washington, D. C., which even at the close of his eight-year administration, in 1809, numbered but 8000 people.

Future Presidents

When *Lincoln* delivered his first inaugural address, Stephen A. Douglas, his long-time rival in politics and love, held his hat. Another notable fact was that in the audience were four future presidents: Hayes, Garfield, Arthur, and Benjamin Harrison.

A "Turn-Coat" President

Old Mr. Dent, *Grant's* father-in-law, lived at the White House until his death in 1873. He came from Missouri and was a staunch Democrat. He called President Grant a "turncoat." Grant's only vote before becoming President was for Buchanan in 1856.

Loud Speakers

Loud speakers were used for the first time at the inauguration of Harding in 1921.

A President in a Hurry

Theodore Roosevelt shaved every day at 12:40; the barber always came to the White House. Teddy was in such a hurry to leave Washington, that he did not complete the inaugural parade with Taft.

Only President from Washington

Grant was the only president to be elected from Washington, D. C. He took up his residence there at the close of the Civil War. His home on Minnesota Row was the gift of an admiring public.

A Proud Mother

Garfield's mother was the first mother of a president to see her son inaugurated. As soon as he took the oath of office, he turned and affectionately kissed her. This simple act of courtesy and devotion won him many friends.

PHYSICAL

What President Accidentally Lost an Eye While in the White House?

Theodore Roosevelt was a marvelous athlete. He entered the White House the youngest president, at the age of forty-one. He was a wrestler, boxer, tennis player, hunter of big game, a crack rifle shot, and one of the best horsemen America ever produced.

His favorite indoor sport was boxing and he was ready to take on all comers. One day he was having a friendly bout with a young naval officer, one of Mrs. Roosevelt's relatives. The lieutenant shot a gloved hand at Roosevelt's face. Teddy dodged, but received a glancing blow on the left eye, rupturing a small blood vessel.

Floating spots appeared a few days later, and Roosevelt's physician was called. He said to the President, "I am sorry, sir, but you have injured your eye, and unless you cease your strenuous exercise, such as wrestling and boxing, you will lose the sight entirely." Teddy replied, "I can't do that, I have an appointment to box this morning, and take a jiu-jitsu lesson this afternoon."

This was in 1904. By 1908 he completely lost the sight of his left eye. He never told anyone, and it was not until thirteen years after the accident, when he wanted to organize a regiment for the World War that he casually made known one day to some newspaper reporters, that he had lost an eye while in the White House. This spirit of consideration has rarely been equalled. The reason Roosevelt kept the affliction a secret for so many years was because he did not wish to hurt the feelings and standing of the

44

young naval officer who had unintentionally caused the injury.

What President Had an Artificial Jaw?

In June, 1893, three months after his second inauguration, *Cleveland* became afflicted with a painful ulceration in the roof of his mouth. When he was informed it was cancer he demanded an immediate operation, providing it would be a secret one. As the country well remembered the death of Grant from cancer, only eight years before, and was now in the midst of a financial panic, the news of a sick president might have a bad effect on the country.

On June 30th, the president boarded a private yacht in New York harbor. During a six-day voyage in Long Island Sound a portion of his upper jaw was removed, care being taken to avoid external scars. Arriving at Buzzard's Bay the President walked ashore unassisted.

About two weeks later another operation was performed to remove remaining diseased tissue. Shortly afterward a prominent New York dentist fitted the president with an artificial upper jaw of vulcanized rubber. It caused no impairment of speech, and no one except the physicians knew that the operation had been performed until ten years after the President's death.

How Did Franklin D. Roosevelt Become Crippled?

In 1920 when *Franklin D. Roosevelt* attended the Democratic national convention in San Francisco, he snatched the New York banner from the Tammany leaders and joined in the wild parade around the hall in honor of Woodrow Wilson. He was only thirty-eight, and a tower of physical strength. The then

Assistant Secretary of the Navy received the nomination for the Vice-Presidency at this convention.

In 1921, while rebuilding his law practice in New York city, he joined his family at Campo Bello Island, in New Brunswick, Canada. Overjoyed at the sight of their father, the children led him in a two-mile run across country. This was immediately followed by a long swim in the icy waters of the Bay of Fundy. He became exhausted, and in three days his magnificent body was twisted with infantile paralysis. At thirty-nine he was crippled from the waist down. It was a cruel misfortune, but did not blight his future.

He is a proficient swimmer and regained his strength at Warm Springs, Georgia. He swims almost daily in the White House pool.

Who Was Our Most Friendly President?

McKinley had few equals in the number of personal friendships. He had a magnetic personality, and no one forgot his cordial handshake, even those whom he refused positions. When he was unable to give an appointment to such an office seeker, he would remove a white carnation from the ever-filled vase on his desk, and pin it on the coat of the visitor. With a reassuring pat on the shoulder he quietly accompanied the caller to the door, and, although disappointed in not getting his job, the man remained a lifelong friend of the president.

While governor of Ohio, he lived at the old Neil Hotel, opposite the capitol. Every morning, before ascending the steps of the state house, he would turn and wave to his invalid wife. Each afternoon at 3:00 o'clock, regardless of official duties, he would go to his office window and wave his handkerchief to his awaiting wife.

What President?

At 49 married a girl of 22.
Had an artificial jaw.
Once hanged a man.
So fussy over details he often answered White
    House phone.
Never visited Washington until he went there
    as President.

(See page 10.)

What President Failed to Visit the White House Office for Seventeen Months?

Wilson was found unconscious on a bathroom floor of the White House on October 4, 1919, soon after his famous western trip in defense of the League of Nations. He was paralyzed on the left side. For months, no one was allowed in the sick room but the doctors, nurses and his devoted wife, who was constantly at his side. Tumulty, his secretary, very rarely saw him, and his real condition was kept from the public.

Mrs. Wilson made many important decisions during her husband's illness.

Later, when strength began to return to the sick president, he was moved about the private rooms in a wheel-chair. Mrs. Wilson carefully arranged every diversion that would tend toward relaxation.

The President greatly loved moving pictures. A private showing of the latest films was staged every afternoon for his special benefit, in the East Room, during 1920 and 1921. Moving picture producers co-operated in every way possible and more than 400 films were shown, many of them first run productions.

For five months after his collapse, he lay a shattered, helpless wreck. In February, 1920, he was able to make his first motor trip. After retiring from office, Wilson went to his private home in Washington, where he was a neighbor to Herbert Hoover.

What President Slept Eleven Hours a Day?

Coolidge was a man whose personality was little known to those not close to him. He was reserved, his affections deep, and he was especially thoughtful of others. But to many the orderliness and plainness of his life were misunderstood.

Coolidge had never owned a car until he became president, had lived in rented homes, and had never ridden in a Pullman until he became vice president. He averaged nine hours of sleep a night, and his afternoon naps were from two to four hours.

This excessive sleeping may have been a sign of ill health, for it was apparent that Coolidge left the presidency a very tired man. He had deeply grieved over the death of his son, while in the White House, and remarked to a friend that presidential life had lost its luster. His old law partner, in Northampton, mentioned that he could notice the great difference in his physical strength after his return from Washington. Coolidge had said, in his last year in the White House, "I do not choose to run in 1928." Those nearest him knew that ill health was probably the reason.

What Pioneer President Had False Teeth Carved from Rhinoceros Ivory?

Washington was a constant sufferer of dental troubles from early youth until his death. He wrote repeatedly in his diary of trouble with his teeth.

At the close of the Revolutionary War, Washington became acquainted with a French dentist who had but recently immigrated to New York. The doctor visited the General at Mt. Vernon, and after several attempts produced a set of false teeth from rhinoceros ivory. They were heavy, unnaturally shaped, and held together by spiral springs. Port wine was used to discolor them and sealing wax to simulate gums. Dr. Greenwood made several such sets for the President shortly before his death.

Needless to say, the false teeth were uncomfortable, often failed to stay in place, and kept the wearer constantly conscious of their presence. Therefore it is not surprising that Washington, who always took great pride in his personal appearance, was reticent about speaking in public.

Everyone has noticed in Washington's portraits his stern expression. This was not intentional, but caused by his ill fitting teeth. But in the old home of John Adams in Quincy, Massachusetts, is an oil painting of Washington made while he was president. In this the facial expression is soft and kindly. The painter, Gilbert Stuart, actually portrayed the real president, for he had removed the false teeth and padded the General's cheeks and lips in order to overcome the sagging lines and hollows.

A curious set of false teeth exhibited at the World's Fair, in Chicago, in 1933, caused much interest. They were once worn by Washington.

What President Had His Clothes Stolen While Swimming in the Potomac River?

John Q. Adams was one of the pioneer athletes of the White House and in the summer often took an early morning swim in the Potomac River. His administration was before the days of private bodyguards, so the President always went unattended, leaving his clothes on the river bank. A tramp came along on one such occasion, spied the garments, and not knowing to whom they belonged, and, caring still less, made off with shirt, pants, money and shoes.

Soon Adams came out of the water and hunted in vain for his clothing. Realizing that it would be embarrassing indeed for the President of the United States to be caught in such a predicament, he wisely decided that the safest place would be back in the water. So back he went and waited until he saw a small boy going fishing. To him he called, "Say, boy, run to the White House, and tell Mrs. Adams to send

a suit of clothes to the President. I'll wait for you."
Yes, John Q. Adams was one of the most dignified
of presidents and was later to become known as
"Old Man Eloquent," but he certainly might have
needed all his dignity and all his eloquence that
morning.

What President Weighed Less Than 100 Pounds?

Madison was the smallest president in stature—
but five feet, four inches in height. He had been an
ailing child and later had to withdraw from Princeton because of critical illness. Contrary to expecta-
tions, he lived to the age of 85, becoming the second
oldest president.

Madison was primarily a student and for most of
his life was dependent on others. Until 50 years of
age he lived with his father on the extensive Mont-
pelier estate now owned by the Du Ponts, in Orange
County, Virginia. Thomas Jefferson, of whom Madison was an ardent student, lived but a few miles
away.

Who Was the Most Unhappy President?

John Adams was perhaps our most unhappy president despite the fact that his political life was highly
successful. He was a co-author and a defender of
the Declaration of Independence. He represented
us in France during the Revolution. He borrowed
money from Holland, when the credit of the thirteen
colonies hung in the balance. He was our first ambassador to England. He was the only man to serve
eight years as vice-president, and then become president. He was the only president who ever saw his
son become president, and yet he was unhappy.

His proud nature did not like being overshadowed

**What President Had His Clothes Stolen While
Swimming in the Potomac River?**

(See page 10.)

by the great character of Washington. Although he was supremely fitted for his high office, and although everyone acknowledged his ability, yet he did not have the faculty of making warm personal friends. He broke with the Federalist party, and they never elected another as president.

Even at the time of his inauguration, he resented it keenly that the citizens should make so great a demonstration in honor of the out-going president and show so little enthusiasm regarding his entry into office.

What President Often Fell Asleep During Important Conferences?

When *Taft* was inaugurated he weighed 332 pounds. He got stuck in the White House bath tub and an extra large tub was installed, particularly for his use.

He was a heavy eater and often fell asleep after a big meal, while engaged in a table conversation. He would often sleep for 15 minutes, then wake up and resume the conversation, only to fall asleep again.

An artist, while painting the President's portrait, looked up to see that his subject had fallen asleep. He complained to an attendant that he found it difficult to paint a picture of a sleeping president.

What President Had Smallpox While in Office?

Lincoln was easily accessible to those who had grievances or were in trouble. A woman, on pretense of pleading for pardon for her son, visited Lincoln immediately after coming from the sick bed of a smallpox patient.

Lincoln contracted the dread disease and was confined to bed for several weeks. His physicians made light of the condition, saying that it was but a mild case of varioloid, but in reality it was a true case of smallpox.

WHITE HOUSE

What President Gave Away 1400 Pounds of Cheese in One Day?

Jackson was one of the most hated, as well as most beloved, of the presidents. Some of his New York state friends presented him with a 1400-pound cheese, which was received in December, preceding his retirement from office. It was on display in the corridor of the White House for several weeks. Jackson was now a widower, well advanced in years, and that much cheese would have lasted him a lifetime; so, on Washington's birthday he made known that all visitors would be welcome at the White House and each should receive a piece of the famous cheese.

The Democrats took it as a joke and passed the word along. An excursion was run from Baltimore, and several thousand people lined up in front of the White House for a piece of the cheese. Of course, Jackson had not expected that so many would accept the invitation, but did not turn them away. When the doors were opened in the morning a motley swarm of visitors entered. They pushed the aged President back against the wall, and every one, in a happy mood, proceeded to dig into the cheese. Some brought knives, forks or spoons, but most of them, having come unprepared, dug in with their fingers. Within a few hours the enormous cheese was carried away by the hilarious throng, who left only a small portion for the President's use. This was perhaps the most unique farewell party ever given by an outgoing president.

Where Was the Declaration of Independence During the Burning of Washington?

In 1814 the City of Washington was captured and the government buildings burned by the British. On the approach of the enemy, an assistant in the secretary of state's office rescued the Declaration of Independence and the Constitution, placed the documents in a gunny sack and fled across the Potomac. That night the sack was hidden in the ruins of an old mill, and later taken to Leesburg, Virginia, until the British left the capital.

Other objects of national interest were also removed, among them the large painting of George Washington, which now hangs in the East Room of the White House. The portrait was rescued by Mrs. Dolly Madison in her flight from Washington, a few hours prior to the arrival of the British.

When Was a $500 Wedding Cake Served in the White House?

Several months after *Wilson's* inauguration, his daughter, Jessie, was married to Francis Sayre, a professor at Princeton University. She was the thirteenth bride to be married in the White House.

The wedding cake had been made in New York. It was in two layers, had a maximum height of two and one-half feet, and a diameter of three feet. It weighed one hundred and thirty-five pounds and cost $500.

Seven hundred guests were invited to the wedding. Among the gifts were two washtubs, six boxes of soap, coal buckets, a barrel of potatoes, five bushels of onions and a twenty-five hundred dollar diamond necklace, presented by the members of the House of Representatives.

What President Gave Away 1400 Pounds of Cheese in One Day?

(See page 10.)

Pioneer Women

During *Madison's* administration, prior to the War of 1812, there were many social attractions in Washington. Many ladies made journeys of great length and hardship to be present during the winter sessions of Congress.

The president's house was then the people's palace. The weekly levees were open to all who chose to come.

A daughter of a senator rode 500 miles on horseback with her father. The wife of another came 1500 miles, traveling through vast forests and Indian settlements.

What President Got Lost in the Woods on His Way to Washington?

In 1800 the seat of the United States Government was still in Philadelphia, but was soon to be transferred to Washington. In November of that year *John Adams* and his wife Abigail set out for the new capitol, following an established stage coach road as far as Baltimore and thereafter pushing through the woods over little used trails. As the couple neared their destination they became lost, but fortunately met a negro who knew the region. He informed them that they were fully eight miles from their route, and volunteered to escort them to the village of Washington, then known as "The City of the Wilderness."

That first administration in Washington is vividly described by Mrs. Adams in her diary. She states that hers was a rigorous life, for the winter was raw, and her own days busy, but lonely. The first lady found the President's Mansion hard to heat and complained of lack of wood for the eleven fireplaces, and though there was much wood to cut, there was no one to cut it. Consequently she and the President lived in six rooms. The environs were swampy and there was much ague and malaria.

Mrs. Adams did her own work and on Monday hung the washing in what is now the famous East Room, from the windows of which could be seen the Capitol being erected in the distance, and the home of her nearest neighbor, a half mile away.

When Was the Key to the White House Dining Room Lost?

Early in 1862, a White House reception was given by *Lincoln* for some very distinguished guests. A magnificent supper had been provided by a steward from New York, but in his over anxiety to keep the crowd out of the dining room until the dinner was served, he locked the door and mislaid the key. Great was the consternation of the crowd when they learned the repast was ready, but could not be reached. After considerable confusion the key was found, the door opened and the hungry crowd fed.

What Recent President Had Twenty Sheep Pastured on the White House Lawn?

As soon as Congress declared war with Germany, *Mrs. Wilson* closed the White House to visitors and locked the gates to the public, admitting only those who had definite appointments.

In keeping with the national spirit she procured twenty blooded sheep and had them pastured on the White House lawn. In this manner the grass was kept in order and a profitable crop of wool produced. At shearing time ninety pounds of wool was obtained and approximately two pounds sent to each state, where it was sold to liberal bidders. More than fifty-two thousand dollars was thus made available to the Red Cross. The proceeds of the second shearing, almost as profitable, were turned over to the Salvation Army for its war work.

What President's Horse Was Pastured on the White House Lawn?

During the Mexican War, *General Zachary Taylor* was served by a single horse, "Old Whitey." Soon after the war Taylor was elected president and took to Washington with him many reminders of his long military life, among them his old mount. Visitors were surprised and pleased to find the old veteran pastured on the White House lawn, totally oblivious to his privilege and the renown of his master.

The visitors liked to take a hair from "Old Whitey's" tail, as a souvenir. The old horse outlived his master, however, and was led in the funeral procession, immediately behind the hearse.

When Did a President Write a Reprieve to Save the Life of a Turkey?

When *Lincoln* began his first term as president, his son, Tad, was only nine, and after the death of his older brother, Willie, became quite a favorite. The boy frequently gathered groups of street urchins of all descriptions and marched them into the White House kitchen for a feast, much to the consternation of the cook.

Tad, like his father, loved animals. The boy had a team of goats and a little wagon which he used to drive around the White House grounds. Visitors were sometimes surprised to see this team hitched to a chair, or being driven at a wild gallop down the corridors of the White House.

A live turkey had been sent to the White House for the Thanksgiving dinner. Soon the big bird was following the boy around and as the feast day approached the child became troubled over the thought of losing his new friend. He was so disturbed over this matter that he approached his father who inter-

rupted an important meeting in order to write a re-
prieve to save the turkey's life. This Tad gleefully
carried to the cook and stayed the execution and the
turkey became one of the permanent household pets.

What President Was Burned in Effigy on the White House Lawn?

Tyler had vetoed the Bank Bill in 1842, much to the
disgust of his Cabinet and the people. A large and
hissing crowd appeared one evening on the White
House lawn and burned him in effigy. The anger
against Tyler was shown by the members of the
Cabinet, all resigning except Webster.

When Tyler left Washington he drove to the Potomac pier ready to take a boat down the river for his
home in Williamsburg. The steamer was just pulling
away when cries of "Ex-President Tyler desires to
go on board," were heard. The river captain, a loyal
Whig, shouted back, "Ex-President Tyler be blazed,
let him take the next boat."

What President Had to Flee from Washington for His Life?

On August 29th, 1814, during the War of 1812,
the British entered Washington soon after their victory at Bladensburg, a few miles away. The city was
defenseless except for a few government clerks who
fired a quick volley and then retreated into Virginia.
President Madison fled and concealed himself in a
hut in a woods some seventeen miles from Washington.

The British marched into the city, burned the
Capitol, the State and Treasury Buildings, the Navy
Yards, and then advanced to the Presidential Mansion. It was fired by the use of a live coal from a
neighboring tavern and Admiral Cockburn, the Brit-

Guess What President

Weighed less than one hundred pounds.
Fled from Washington for his life.
Was supported by his father until he was fifty.
A shorthand expert.
Went home from college to die.
Lived to be our second oldest President.

(See page 10.)

ish commander, ate his supper, or rather Madison's supper, by the light of the blazing building.

A violent storm and heavy thunder shower put out the fires, and the British left the city, as quietly as they had entered. Three days later Madison and his wife returned to find their beautiful mansion a mass of smoldering ruins. Part of the walls were still standing, however, and the building was later rebuilt of Virginia sandstone, along the original lines. When completed some of the sandstone showed the black marks of the fire and these were hidden by painting the entire structure white. It thereafter became known as the "White House."

What President's Will Disappeared for Many Years?

Washington was our wealthiest president. At his death, his wealth, exclusive of the Mt. Vernon estate of 8000 acres, was $530,000.

Early in 1800 his will was filed for probate in Fairfax county court house, Virginia. To everyone's surprise it was found that the 24-page document was prepared by himself and signed but six months before his death. In it he decreed that his wife should have life estate and that at her death all his slaves should receive their freedom.

The will reposed in the files of the court house until the Civil War, when it was removed to Richmond for safety. At the close of the war it mysteriously disappeared, but was eventually returned, much the worse for wear. Naturally such a document aroused public interest and constant handling and the pinning together of the now fragile sheets made it difficult to read. The authorities, with the best of intentions, gave it to an inexperienced woman to mend, but she returned it in even worse condition.

Finally it was suggested that because of the great value of the document, it should be sent to Washington and repaired by experts. However, local authorities refused to sanction its removal. Great agitation continued and it was thought that the Virginia legislature would have to pass an act to make possible the loan of the document to the Congressional Library long enough for repairs. Finally a compromise was made and an expert was sent to Fairfax Court House with complete equipment for its restoration.

What President Paid $800 for a Set of Harness?

Buchanan, the predecessor of Lincoln, our only bachelor president, spared neither money nor effort to maintain an elegant style of living.

He used a magnificent carriage, and his handsome span of horses was well worth seeing. A set of harness, which was intended as a gift from a Philadelphia firm, was brought to the White House, with the intention of presenting it to the President. It was truly magnificent, for there were thirty-six buckles heavily plated with silver and fifty-six "B's."

But Buchanan had made it a policy to never accept gifts. Thus, upon inquiry as to the cost of the harness, he wrote his check for $800.

When Did a White House Banquet Cost $40.00 Per Plate?

During the *Grant* administration the White House was a center of hospitality. The public receptions had an informality that pleased every one and both the official and less formal dinners were eagerly anticipated. The General was congenial, Mrs. Grant was a perfect hostess, and the food served by a famous Italian steward, the first White House steward since the days of Dolly Madison, was of excellent repute.

Social life in Washington was greatly revived and Grant's administration was considered the gayest and brightest in many years. The Grant family had been through poverty, had had a severe taste of the horrors of war and thus were warm-hearted and hospitable.

The White House table seated only 36 guests, so regular banquets were given with exactly this number of invitations. Some of these dinners cost as little as $300, but the usual amount was $700. A state banquet was given for Prince Arthur of England for which the cost was $1500, exclusive of the wines.

What President Had Twenty-Four Wagonloads of Old Furniture Hauled Away from the White House?

Arthur, who possessed a beautiful home in New York, refused to live in the White House after Garfield's death, until it was put in better condition. The furniture was worn and soiled, the china chipped and marred and hangings and carpets needed cleaning or replacing. The storerooms and attics were filled with odds and ends of discarded furniture and left-overs from former administrations. There were forgotten toys, cast-off clothing, old umbrellas, rat traps, rubbish of every description, and a great assortment of gifts which former presidents did not see fit to take with them. Such an accumulation was considered a fire hazard.

Twenty-four wagonloads of household goods of all descriptions were hauled away and sold at auction. A pair of trousers and a battered silk hat, formerly belonging to Lincoln, were part of the collection. A beautiful sideboard which had been presented to Mrs.

Hayes by the ladies of the W. C. T. U. was also auctioned and, ironically enough, was purchased by a prominent Washington saloon keeper, who loaded it with wines and liquors and placed it in his bar room. Relic hunters had their fill, and carried away the various articles in high glee. Even a rat-trap, that had caught the famous rat that ate up part of Lincoln's suit, was sold for a high price. This, the first sale of cast-off articles from the White House since Buchanan's administration, 25 years before, netted a total of three thousand dollars.

Who Was the Greatest White House Mistress?

Dolly Madison, as she was affectionately called, was one of the most popular First Ladies of the White House. She was beautiful, witty and possessed the supreme art of making all her visitors feel perfectly at home. Madison had few personal charms, but his wife made up for his weakness in meeting the public.

After her husband's death, Mrs. Madison lived in Washington, a block from the White House, and many a statesman, after calling on the new president, would pay his respects to "Queen Dolly." She died at eighty-two, shortly after her last appearance, at the British Embassy where she dined with Henry Clay and Daniel Webster.

Most presidents' wives were soon forgotten after the death of their husbands, but not so with Mrs. Madison.

Carries Off White House Files

When *President Johnson* left the White House he took with him all the files of the administration. They contained records of the famous impeachment trial.

What President Was Arrested for Speeding in Washington?

(See page 10.)

When Was the First Bathtub Installed in the White House?

In 1850 *President Fillmore* had the first bathtub installed in the White House and the same facilities were used for approximately 35 years, until the Cleveland administration.

A duplicate of this tub can be seen in President Buchanan's old home, Wheatland, at Lancaster, Pennsylvania. It is about twice the size of a present-day bathtub and was made of sheets of metal, soldered together. Water was doubtless heated on the kitchen stove.

A Dissatisfied Father

While *Fillmore* was President, his father, a venerable gentleman of eighty, made a brief visit at the White House, but soon took his departure. Some friends asked him why he did not stay longer, and he replied, "No, no, I will go, I don't like it here; it isn't a good place to live; it isn't a good place for Millard either; I wish he was at home in Buffalo."

A Dirty White House

After the sudden death of Zachary Taylor, *President Fillmore* took office. He found the White House in a miserable condition, dirty and bare. The great room over the Blue Room was covered with a straw carpet, made filthy by tobacco juice. Old Zachary Taylor loved his tobacco and was not very careful. Mrs. Taylor smoked a corn-cob pipe.

A General Has His Pockets Picked

At one of the White House receptions, held during the administration of *John Q. Adams,* General Winfield Scott had his pocket picked of $800.

A Proud Cook.

When *Hayes* came to the White House he brought with him his old colored cook. When she arrived in Washington, she proclaimed herself, "De fust colored lady of de lan."

A Cook's Difficulties

Mrs. Fillmore had a large range placed in the White House kitchen. The novelty greatly enraged the old colored cook, who had been used to a huge fireplace, with cranes, hooks, pots, kettles and skillets. He had managed to prepare a large state dinner for 36 guests every Thursday in the huge fireplace, but could not manage the drafts of the range.

First Billiard Table

John Q. Adams had the first billiard table in the White House. It was purchased by his son at his own expense. Many of the citizens of Washington were astonished at this form of recreation for the president.

Hand Shaking an Art

McKinley shook hands at the rate of 2500 persons per hour. He had the all-time record. On New Year's Day, 1902, Theodore Roosevelt shook hands with 8100 visitors; in 1906, 8000; and in 1907, 8513.

Chandeliers

During the administration of *Grant*, the great chandeliers of the East Room of the White House were installed. They cost $1,800 each and were made in Germany. Each contained 5060 pieces of cut glass.

Do You Know Him?

Runaway bound boy.
Was a tailor by trade.
Taught to write by his wife.
Entertained 400 children at one party.
Carried away White House files.

(See page 10.)

A Dwarf Visitor

P. T. Barnum brought General Tom Thumb to the White House during *Polk's* administration. The President adjourned a Cabinet meeting for a visit with the famous midget.

Fast Music

Fast military music was played by the Marine Band, under instructions of *Theodore Roosevelt*, whenever he wanted the long lines of guests to move quickly at a White House reception.

A Children's Party

Johnson greatly loved children. He celebrated his 60th birthday in the White House by a large party, at which 400 children were entertained. Mrs. Johnson was an invalid and only appeared at two White House receptions. Her life in Washington was not a happy one. She said she was far more content when her husband was a tailor.

The First Movie

The first motion picture ever shown in the White House was in 1912. A movietone film was shown in December, 1927, six months before the first talking pictures were released. Coolidge read his 1928 Thanksgiving proclamation into a newsreel microphone.

A President Drives a Cow

When *William Henry Harrison* became president, he needed a cow. The next Saturday he went to market and purchased a good Durham. He assisted the farmer in driving the cow to the White House stables through the main streets of Washington.

A Bicycle in the East Room

It is said that young Webb Hayes, the 20-year-old Secretary of *President Hayes*, learned to ride a bicycle in the famous East Room of the White House.

A Cow Pasture

Mrs. Taft purchased a Jersey cow and allowed it to be pastured on the White House lawn, much to the interest and amusement of foreign guests.

A Democratic President

While *Jefferson* was President, he greatly offended a British Minister by receiving him while wearing his house-slippers.

Did Not Enjoy the Theatre

Hoover was not an enthusiast about the theatre and did not attend at any time during his four-year occupancy of the White House.

Huge Wine Bill

While *Jefferson* was President, he brought eleven servants from Monticello at his own expense. His wine bill for the two administrations was more than $10,000.

What President?

Never saw a map of the United States until
   he was nineteen.
A handsome President.
Installed first bathtub in White House.
Installed first kitchen range in White House.
Installed first library in White House.

(See page 10.)

ACTIVITIES

What President Went from a County Clerk's Office to the White House in One Promotion?

William Henry Harrison, the war hero of 1812, retired to his farm, North Bend, on the Ohio River near Cincinnati. He previously had been Governor of the Northwest Territory and now his county elected him to the office of clerk of courts. In 1840 the Whigs elected him to the presidency in the famous Log Cabin and Hard Cider Campaign.

Harrison was the oldest president, taking office at the age of 68. He was also the first president to die in office, his death taking place but a month after his inauguration. Although he was given an imposing funeral in Washington, the public failed to mark his grave for many years. But today a beautiful monument marks his resting place at his old home near Cincinnati.

What President Spent 32 Years in Building a 33-Room House?

Jefferson cut the timbers himself, burned his own brick, and had the necessary nails manufactured on his plantation. The mansion, when finally completed, had 33 rooms, including twelve bedrooms and ten rooms in the basement. Truly, a large home for a widower, but here he entertained his guests, made a home for his children and his many grandchildren, and received a host of visitors.

74

What President Was Also an Inventor?

Jefferson was perhaps the most versatile of presidents. In addition to having the requisites normally expected of an executive, he was a practical inventor, an amateur astronomer, an author, linguist, and musician.

Jefferson's practical inventions were a letter-copying press, a hemp machine, a swivel chair, a folding chair, and a folding ladder. The automatic closing doors of the type used today in streetcars are modeled from his plans. Farmers are indebted to his experimentation, for the modern plow has been perfected from the one with which he took first prize at a Paris Exposition.

Pure science intrigued him. He constructed a pedometer to measure the distance covered on his walks, and built on his front porch a weather vane, which could be read either from the inside or outside of the house. He was surgeon enough to set the broken leg of a slave. He was mathematician enough to calculate an eclipse, and when past eighty years of age he set up one of the first astronomical telescopes in the United States.

The versatile Jefferson knew French, German, Spanish, Italian, Latin, and Greek. Still he found time to write three books of a political nature. An accomplished musician, his violin helped to pass many a lonely hour.

A Runaway President

A reward was once offered for the return of *President Johnson* when he was a penniless, runaway apprentice boy from North Carolina.

What President Once Hanged a Man?

Cleveland began his public career as Sheriff of

Buffalo, Erie County, New York. As part of his duties he hanged a murderer rather than assign the unpleasant task to a deputy.

Three years before his election to the presidency Cleveland was not known outside the limits of his own county. He had never visited Washington until he attended his own inaugural.

Cleveland was, perhaps, the hardest working president. He toiled late at night, writing his letters laboriously, in longhand. Fussy over details, he often insisted on answering the White House phone. Contrastingly he was careless of his personal appearance, and was an inveterate chewer of tobacco.

Cleveland was not an orator, not a good mixer, and had a mechanical handshake. However, he was absolutely honest and courageous. One of his first duties as president was to measure the hay in the White House stables and send a check to his predecessor for it.

Cleveland's daughter, Esther, was the only president's child to be born in the White House. The south gate was once open to the public, but Mrs. Cleveland ordered it locked, because too many strangers stopped to kiss the baby.

What President, While in Office, Sold His Private Business for Almost a Half Million Dollars?

Harding was editor of the *Marion Star* in Marion, Ohio, and while President sold the paper for $480,000. He was our first business man president, and at his death left an estate of $930,444.54.

Of our thirty-one presidents, twenty-three were lawyers, four were soldiers: Grant, Washington, William H. Harrison and Taylor. Woodrow Wilson was a college president; Herbert Hoover, a mining

engineer; and strangest of all, we had one trades-
man, Andrew Johnson, the tailor.

Wounded Presidents

Of the sixteen presidents who saw military service, only Hayes and Monroe were wounded in battle.

What President Was Also a Preacher?

Garfield worked his way through Hiram College,
near Cleveland, eventually becoming its president.
He was an ordained minister of the Church of
Christ, and a great favorite at its camp meetings
and revivals.

While associated with the college he studied law
in his spare time, passed the bar examination, and
then took up politics as his life work. Noted for his
eloquence, he often preached in Washington while
still a congressman and prior to his election as president.

Hobbies

Franklin D. Roosevelt enjoys stamp-collecting as
a hobby. He has over 20,000 specimens in his collection.

Jefferson gave us the system of dimes and dollars.

Washington and *Lincoln* were both surveyors at
one time in their lives.

What President Established a Botanical Garden?

John Quincy Adams was a great student of horti-
culture and established a botanical garden in Washington. Naval officers were instructed to bring home,
for distribution, the seeds of such grains and vegetables as they might deem desirable to naturalize in

Who Is This?

Only lived one month in office.
Died from exposure to cold.
Drove his cow to the White House.
Went from county clerk's office to Presidency
in one promotion.

(See page 10.)

this country. The seeds thus collected were distributed through members of Congress and several important varieties of vegetables were thus introduced. Through many years, the distribution of seeds to rural constituents, by congressmen, was an established custom.

What President, While in Office, Marched at the Head of an Army?

The excise tax of 1791 placed a revenue of seven cents per gallon on whiskey. This was resented by the farmers in four counties, south of Pittsburgh, where stills were numerous. They organized, besieged the home of the local revenue officer, and defied the Government to collect the tax.

Washington saw it was time to show the strength of the National Government, so, in 1794, he called for volunteers from Virginia, Maryland and Eastern Pennsylvania to march to the vicinity of Pittsburgh. Thirteen thousand men were formed into companies and moved westward, Washington marching with them for six days.

The actual purpose of the army was to overawe the rioters, not to fight, and the results were everything that had been hoped. The insurgents saw that the Government actually meant business, and most of them fled westward before the army arrived.

What President Was Known for His Night Parties?

Arthur was a widower, handsome, an excellent entertainer, and the best dressed president. He was a man of the world, a lover of night clubs, and one who considered his private life his own affair.

A man of good taste and careful personal appearance, Arthur was said to have had, at a single time, eighty pairs of trousers with other clothes to match. Furthermore, he was a master of etiquette, possessing the faculty of immediately putting his guests at their ease.

Arthur's White House dinners were famed for their elegance of service, and the excellence of the food. On March 8th, 1882, Arthur gave a very fine party to twenty guests. The state dining room had been wonderfully decorated and banked with flowers. The guests were seated at 7:30 and the fourteen-course dinner completed at 10:00.

Arthur's heavy eating, drinking and continuous round of parties brought on Bright's Disease. He died at his New York home, less than two years after retirement.

When Was a Thousand Dollars Bet on a President's Golf Score?

During the first years of the twentieth century the Myopia Golf Course, at Boston, was considered one of the most difficult in the country. Any one who could play the course under a score of 100 could well be proud of his achievement.

In accordance with a bet of a thousand dollars, *President Taft* set out one August morning, in 1909, to shoot the course under the specified hundred strokes. To his own surprise, the giant president turned in his card at 98. He was so jubilant that he kissed his wife in public.

Despite his great weight Taft was a very active man. As a student at Yale, he was a noted wrestler, and rowed stroke on the varsity crew. While Commissioner General of the Philippine Islands he weighed over 300 pounds, yet his favorite exercise was horseback riding.

What President Liked to Walk?

Theodore Roosevelt was a great walker and often planned what he called obstacle walks for his sons. He would often invite visitors at the White House to accompany the group, not revealing what was in store for them.

Ambassador Jusserand once went on one of these trips by invitation. Roosevelt led a lively clip, observing the rule "Over or through, but never around." Teddy waded through a pond and the willing ambassador followed, shoes and all. Later the bedraggled Frenchman completed the walk but still wore his gloves, for he said, he might meet the ladies.

Other presidents were famous walkers, among them Benjamin Harrison and Arthur. Harrison enjoyed walking as much as ten miles at a time, usually starting out, unaccompanied, at ten o'clock in the evening.

Arthur always walked at night, usually with a congenial friend and sometimes until the early hours of the morning.

What Pioneer President Personally Wrote 25,000 Letters During His Lifetime?

Jefferson was an incessant letter writer, and had very little use for private secretaries. This, of course, was before the days of typewriters, when all letters were written by hand. In order to keep a record of any promise made or statement given he invented a letter copying press.

During his seventeen years in retirement, at Monticello, his correspondence steadily increased. Aspirants for political honors wrote to Jefferson, knowing that they would always receive a reply. Many young students wrote merely to obtain the autograph of the famous ex-president.

Jefferson had a peculiar human interest in people, and all of his letters were so characterized, especially those to his children, grandchildren and personal friends. Likewise his cultural side unconsciously showed itself in all of his public and private writings.

ODDITIES

Defeated Presidents

Most people believe that a President of the United States has a steady rise to power, and that he climbs the ladder of success without a single reverse. The biographies of the presidents note that more than half suffered defeats.

Lincoln was defeated for United States senator. But had he been elected senator, he might not have been president during the Civil War.

Benjamin Harrison was defeated for United States senator and for governor of Indiana.

Harding was defeated for governor of Ohio.

McKinley was defeated for re-election to Congress, after 14 years of faithful service.

Grant, facing court martial, resigned from the army prior to the Civil War.

Polk was twice defeated for governor of Tennessee.

Jackson was defeated for president in 1824.

Madison was defeated for the Virginia legislature.

Wm. H. Harrison was recalled while minister to Columbia, South America.

Buchanan was twice defeated for the Democratic nomination for president.

Fillmore was defeated for governor of New York.

Cleveland was defeated for prosecuting attorney at Buffalo.

Van Buren was recalled while minister to England.

Arthur was discharged as collector of the port of New York.

Theodore Roosevelt was defeated for mayor of New York City.

Do You Know Him?

Had 80 pairs of trousers.
Loved night parties.
Had 24 wagonloads of furniture hauled away
   from White House.
Died less than two years after retirement.
Once served a 14-course dinner.

(See page 10.)

Coolidge was defeated for school board in North-ampton, Massachusetts.

Hoover had a defeat for the Republican nomination before his election.

Franklin D. Roosevelt was defeated for vice-president in 1920.

Monroe was recalled while minister to France.

All these were defeated, yet they became presidents of the United States. Our country loves a good loser, someone that can take it on the chin and come up smiling. While these men were defeated for minor offices, yet they persisted, and each won the pearl of greater price—the presidency of the United States.

Ages of the Presidents

The pioneer presidents appeared to live longer than the later ones. John Adams lived to be *91,* his son, John Q. Adams, *81.* Jefferson lived to be *83,* and Madison, *85.* Compare this record with the ages of our later presidents:

Garfield assassinated at *50;* Lincoln assassinated at *56;* McKinley assassinated at *58;* Theodore Roosevelt found dead in bed at *61;* Coolidge dropped dead at *61;* and Harding died suddenly at *58.*

The first six presidents lived to an average age of *79.*

The last six died at an average age of only *62.*

What President Caused the German Kaiser to Change His Mind?

While *Theodore Roosevelt* was president, the German government was at the point of seizing some territory in Venezuela, as a security for claims. Roosevelt told the German ambassador that if the Kaiser did not submit to arbitration within ten days,

Admiral Dewey would be sent to stop the Germans from landing their troops. The minister protested, saying that the Kaiser could not back down. Roosevelt replied that he was not responsible for the Kaiser's actions, but wanted to make it plain what he himself intended to do. After waiting a week the ambassador was informed that the time limit was cut to nine days, and that unless Germany agreed to arbitrate within forty-eight hours, Dewey would sail. In thirty-six hours the ambassador returned and said that the Kaiser consented to arbitrate.

"H" Presidents Never Re-elected

Strange to say, no president whose last name begins with H has ever been re-elected.

Harrison, Wm. H.

Harrison, Benjamin

Hayes

Harding

Hoover

Facial Appearances

It is interesting to note the facial appearances of the various presidents. They reflect the customs of the times in which they lived. For 72 years, up until the time of Lincoln, none of our pioneer presidents wore either a beard or mustache. During the Civil War, it was customary for the officers to wear beards. Consequently the Union generals, who later became presidents—Grant, Hayes, Garfield and Benjamin Harrison—all wore full beards. The custom then changed and Cleveland, Theodore Roosevelt and Taft wore business men's mustaches. More recently the presidents have returned to the custom of the pioneers and are smooth faced, as Wilson, Harding, Coolidge, Hoover and Franklin D. Roosevelt.

What President Caused a Bend in Pennsylvania Avenue?

Jackson cared nothing for formality. He was a widower while president, and lived his life in his own way. During his term the treasury offices were being rebuilt, after the burning of Washington. After much argument, the matter was left to his decision as to the exact location of the building. Surveyors had set their tripods in various places and yet, no one could decide. Jackson, in much disgust, vigorously poked his cane into the loose earth and said without a moment's hesitation, "Put the corner-stone right here," and quickly left the scene. This was where the corner-stone was finally placed. The building was ultimately completed and it is for this reason that Pennsylvania Avenue is not straight, as originally planned, but curves around the Treasury Building.

Jackson loved fast horses, cock fights, and all-round sports. He had no children of his own, but adopted a nephew and an Indian boy, whose mother had been killed on the battlefield. History places him as one of the most unique characters the White House had ever known. He absolutely knew no fear and this Government was never molested by a foreign nation during his term of office. He not only had two terms of office but he also dictated who his successor should be—Martin Van Buren.

Jackson loved to lie under the trees on the White House lawn, smoking a pipe, much to the disgust of the citizens of Washington.

Most Leading Presidents Did Not Use a Middle Initial

George Washington
Abraham Lincoln
Thomas Jefferson
Andrew Jackson
Theodore Roosevelt
John Adams
James Madison
James Monroe
Woodrow Wilson
Herbert Hoover
William McKinley
Grover Cleveland
Benjamin Harrison
Calvin Coolidge

Comparison of Franklin D. Roosevelt and Theodore Roosevelt

They were distant cousins.
Both children of wealth.
Both of Holland-Dutch descent.
Both graduates of Harvard.
Both overcame physical handicaps.
Both governor of New York state.
Both assistant-secretary of the navy.
Both ran for vice-president.
Both were shot at by a maniac.
Both served two terms as president.

The above was contributed by Earl Hale of Marion, Ohio. Mr. Hale is one of Ohio's best authorities on the lives of the presidents.

Who Is Polk?

When *Polk* was nominated in 1844, he was unknown to most of the nation, and far from being a popular figure. When the news reached a New

England steamboat captain, he shouted, "Hurrah for —what did you say his name was?"

When Was Liquor Served in Congress?

The customs of the senators and representatives, about 1850, were strange indeed. It was common to have wines upon the desks in Congress, and the famous "Hole in the Wall" was constantly patronized by thirsty legislators. Intoxication and disorder were frequent, some of the members being carried out bodily.

Fireplaces, with hickory wood, and old-fashioned Franklin stoves did their share in taking off the wintry chill. But if the stern law-makers remained long at their desks, they wrapped themselves in shawls, which were fastened with large safety pins.

The congressmen wore tall silk hats, side whiskers, eye-glass ribbons, and high stand-up collars. Most of them were users of snuff and pages were kept busy replenishing the supply.

Wilson Breaks a Precedent

Jefferson sent his message to Congress by his secretary. He did this because he had a poor speaking voice. This custom was followed for 112 years until Woodrow Wilson, to the utter amazement of the entire nation, appeared before Congress and personally read his message.

Fire Fighting Presidents

President Fillmore and his Cabinet worked as volunteer firemen during the burning of the old Congressional Library in 1851. John Q. Adams, as president, organized and directed the bucket brigade at the fire in which the Treasury Building was damaged during his administration.

Which President?

Returned home with $90.00 in his pocket.
Gave away 1400 pounds of cheese in one day.
His wife smoked cigars.
Married the same wife twice.
Shot a man in a duel.
Paid off the National debt.
Caused the bend in Pennsylvania Avenue.

(See page 10.)

Most Handsome Presidents.

Fillmore and Harding were considered the most handsome presidents. Van Buren and Arthur were the most polished in manners.

The president is the only government official who need not sign the payroll.

Of our thirty-one presidents, eight were born in Virginia and seven in Ohio. Only one president was born west of the Mississippi River—Herbert Hoover, in Iowa.

Theodore Roosevelt was a much-traveled president. During his first term he traveled 50,000 miles and visited every state in the Union.

Only two presidents were born in large cities— Taft in Cincinnati, and Theodore Roosevelt in New York City.

Tallest President

Jefferson and Washington were the same height, 6 feet, 2 inches. The tallest president was Lincoln, measuring 6 feet, 4 inches. Our shortest president was Madison, 5 feet, 4 inches. Polk was the most slender of the presidents. His coats were all tailored to make him look larger.

What President Was So Little Thought of That His Native State Debated 50 Years Before Building Him a Monument?

Pierce, from New Hampshire, was elected to the presidency in 1852. Oddly, this northern man had southern principles, so it is not surprising that his election was by a large majority. Yet he was little known and his administration proved colorless— typical of the years preceding the Civil War, when there were many brilliant statesmen, but few outstanding presidents.

No school boy ever delivers an oration on Franklin Pierce and even his own state failed to appreciate him. In fact 50 years elapsed before it properly commemorated him with a monument.

A Second-Hand President

Fillmore took office after the sudden death of Zachary Taylor in 1850. He was stately in appearance, but is not regarded as one of the outstanding presidents. An old White House attendant, Edward Moran, went with him one day to look at a fine carriage being sold by a gentleman who was leaving Washington. Fillmore admired it very much and said, "It is fine, Edward, but how would it seem for the President of the United States to be riding around in a second-hand carriage?" Edward replied, "But, you see, your *excellency*, you're only a second-hand president."

A Fit of Temper

While John Adams was president, he became so angry with his own party, that he left the seat of government for three months and let the affairs of the nation run themselves.

Prophecy Fulfilled

In a conversation with John W. Davis, in 1922, Franklin D. Roosevelt prophesied Davis' candidacy for the presidency two years later, and his own candidacy six years later. Both prophesies were fulfilled. These predictions appeared in an article in the *Outlook* magazine, November 5, 1930, two years prior to the Democratic convention which nominated Roosevelt.

Log Cabin Presidents

Six presidents were born in log cabins. They were Jackson, Taylor, Fillmore, Buchanan, Lincoln and Garfield. William Henry Harrison was elected as a log cabin president, but biographers found that he had been born in a beautiful southern mansion on the banks of the James River in Virginia, instead of in a log cabin.

A Mediocre President

Pierce had the only cabinet to remain unchanged for four years. While he was running for president, a stranger visited New Hampshire and asked an old inn keeper what he thought of Franklin Pierce. The old gentleman replied, "Waal, up here, he's right smart of a fellah, but spread him over the whole nation I'm afraid he will be very thin in spots."

Forgets His Appointments

President Taft often forgot his own appointments. A week after his inauguration he made an 11:00 o'clock appointment to meet the Supreme Court. At that same hour he also had an appointment to meet his Cabinet. He never could be hurried.

What President Was Arrested for Speeding in Washington?

Grant was the only president ever arrested during his term of office. He loved fast horses, always had several in the White House stables, and had taken the highest mark for horsemanship in his class at West Point. His record in the high jumps has never been equalled.

One day he was driving a spirited team in Washington, exceeded the speed limit, and was arrested by a colored policeman. The President put up a deposit of $20.00, but never appeared at the police court, and commended the colored policeman for doing his duty.

Irritated Office Seeker

Jackson, the victorious general, once had his nose twisted by an irritated office seeker.

The President Who Remembered

A congressman persuaded President Cleveland to appoint one of his constituents to an office. The President afterwards found the appointee of a bad reputation. Later, when this same congressman called, Cleveland greeted him with a snarl, saying, "Do you want me to appoint another horsethief?"

What State Has Furnished Half the Presidents for the Last 68 Years?

Ohio has given the Nation, by birth, seven presidents since 1869. They are Grant, Hayes, Garfield, Benjamin Harrison, McKinley, Taft, and Harding.

The other seven presidents, since 1869, not born in Ohio, are Arthur, Cleveland, the two Roosevelts, Wilson, Coolidge and Hoover.

What President Saw the Battle of Bunker Hill, Yet Lived to Serve in Congress, with Lincoln?

John Quincy Adams had, perhaps, the longest active public career of any man in American history. As a lad of nine, at his mother's side, he saw the Battle of Bunker Hill. Seventy-one years later he was serving in Congress, with a young man of 37, named Lincoln. His political career began as Secretary to the Russian Legation at 14. After being president, he served in Congress for 18 years and fell with a stroke of paralysis while rising to address the Speaker. He was the only president to die in the Capitol.

Adams was considered the poorest dressed President, wearing the same hat for ten years. He was the only bald-headed president. He was so methodical in his habits that people could set their watches by him. At the age of nine he began his diary and kept it faithfully until his death, at 81. This account consists of twelve printed volumes, and is considered the greatest personal document in all America. He was known as "Old Man Eloquent."

When was Washington Sharply Rebuffed by a Scotchman?

Washington took a great deal of interest in the founding of the District of Columbia. He, at one time, called on Davis Burns, a tight-fisted old Scotchman, who owned the farm where the White House now stands. Washington entreated him for a donation of ground, saying "Had not the Federal City been laid out here, you would have died a poor tobacco planter." Burns quickly replied, "Yes, if it hadn't of been for the Widow Custis and her niggers, you would still have been a surveyor and a very poor one at that." But ultimately the old Scotchman donated the desired piece of ground which is now LaFayette Square.

Guess Who

A mediocre President.

His wife didn't like to live in White House.

His native state debated fifty years before building him a monument.

His son was killed one month after election.

(See page 10.)

RETIREMENT

What President, After Retirement, Almost Went Bankrupt Entertaining His Friends?

Jefferson was a most generous host. After a long career in public service, as secretary of state, president and foreign diplomat, he retired to his country mansion at Monticello, near Charlottesville, Virginia. There he displayed true southern hospitality, entertaining many of his old friends and welcoming new acquaintances.

But curiosity seekers took advantage of Jefferson's friendship. Congressmen and senators from the southern states all managed to arrive at Monticello in time for supper. Young men, seeking political advice, also came for a meal. They ate all his chickens and hogs. A beef would be butchered, but it lasted only a few days. Jefferson's own horses would be crowded from their stables, and still the stream of visitors continued.

His only opportunity for real privacy was during the three months of winter when the roads were impassable, and visitors could not reach Monticello. He never turned anyone away. He had sought retirement, but American citizens beat a path to his door.

There were twelve bedrooms in the mansion, and nearly all were occupied every night. A host of servants was required to prepare the food. He ran a regular tavern, and yet, no one ever offered to pay. The guests would line up on both sides of the long dining-room table, and one would say, "Mr. Jefferson, you're a wonderful man, now pass the fried chicken."

Jefferson was once wealthy, but his last days were sad indeed. In his old age he endorsed for a friend a $20,000 note which he later had to pay. Had it not been for financial aid from loyal friends, he would have died in poverty.

What President, After Retirement, Was Forced to Pawn His Private Possessions for a Loan?

After *Grant* retired from the presidency, he needed a larger income. He was influenced by a young man, named Ward, to form an investment company in New York City.

Grant advanced his personal money, but knew nothing of the business. Profits seemed to come in quickly, and he thought all was well. Ward had used the ex-president's name to obtain credit among wealthy men, and had influenced many Civil War veterans to invest their life savings.

Business went on for three years, Grant having absolute confidence in his partner. But on Sunday, May 4, 1884, Ward appeared at Grant's home, and said that they must raise a large sum of money at once. Grant knew nothing of finance, but went quickly to the home of William H. Vanderbilt where he immediately secured a personal loan of a hundred and fifty thousand dollars. He gave the check to Ward, who pretended to deposit it in the bank, but instead put it in his own pocket.

The Marine National Bank, of New York, closed its doors on May 7, and General Grant was stunned to find that instead of being a millionaire, as he supposed, the firm of Grant and Ward was bankrupt and had overdrawn its account two million dollars.

The entire family had but $80.00 in cash. Grant spent a restless night with visions of poverty in his old age, and long lines of disappointed investors clamoring for their money. He was utterly dejected, and did not have sufficient money to pay tradesmen's bills.

He then gave to Vanderbilt, as security for the loan already made, all of his real estate and personal belongings, including swords and trophies, which had been presented to him by an admiring nation after the war. Eventually Vanderbilt gave these swords and curios to the Government, and they are now on display in the National Museum in Washington.

What President Never Drew His Salary Until He Retired from Office?

The thrifty Dutch President, *Van Buren*, realized he would need money after retirement, therefore he drew his four years' salary, a total of $100,000, at the completion of his term.

He lived at Kinderhook, a village of only 600 people, south of Albany. There he fitted up a very elegant country estate—Lindenwald. Recently $5,-000 was offered for the scenic wall-paper from the old mansion, paper which Van Buren had brought from England. Van Buren left an estate of a quarter of a million dollars, but died in comparative obscurity during the Civil War. In fact, many of the city newspapers made no mention of his death.

Van Buren came into national prominence as a leading champion of Jackson's candidacy for president. He wrote many of Jackson's state papers, for the old General was a very poor speller, and had only a rudimentary education.

Van Buren was suave, diplomatic and clever. He took Burr as his model for intrigue, and for General Jackson he planned and executed some of the most difficult political maneuvers in history. He made attitude and deportment a study. His speeches were polished and his poise excellent. It was noticed during the public auction of his goods that the carpet in front of a large mirror in his study was worn threadbare. That was where he had rehearsed his speeches.

A Weary President

A gentleman visiting Princeton saw ex-President *Cleveland* on his front porch, and stepped in to pay his respects. The gentleman said, "Mr. Cleveland, you must be a very happy man, having retired from politics as you have." Cleveland replied, "On the contrary, I am the most unhappy man in America."

What President Returned Home with Only $90.00 in His Pocket?

Jackson spent almost his entire life in the service of his country. Being so well pleased with his successor, Van Buren, he remained for a brief visit with him in the White House. Then he started on his long trip home to Tennessee, a month-long journey, for the roads were almost impassable in the early spring. While homeward bound he gave away a hundred and fifty silver half dollars to his namesakes. Jackson said that they could "teeth" on them.

"Old Hickory" had thousands of admirers, and his trip home from the White House was a continuous ovation. But as he had retired from the presidency much broken in health and finances he was content to spend the rest of his days at the Hermitage, living a consistent Christian life, and visiting, every day, the grave of his wife, Rachel.

This grand old war hero, once noted for his profanity, fiery temper, and a veteran of four duels, now led in the family prayer every evening. He read a chapter of the Bible, and then led in the singing of a hymn, giving out two lines at a time.

His death was most pathetic. Surrounded by his family, his friends, and his servants, who fairly worshipped him, his last words were: "My dear children, friends and servants, I hope and trust to meet you all in Heaven, both white and black."

What President Retired $20,000 in Debt?

Jefferson could balance the National budget, but could not pay his private debts. He had formerly been a prosperous lawyer, but many years of continuous public service had used up his financial reserve.

He was "land poor", and during his long absence the slaves well nigh devoured all the crops from his plantation. He was a poor financier, and, fearing that his creditors might jail him for debt, at the close of his presidential term, he secured a private loan to pay off his obligations.

What President, at 82, Founded a State University?

Jefferson, at 82, designed the buildings and grounds of the University of Virginia. It was the child of his old age and fitting that it should be located at Charlottesville, but four miles from his home, where its construction could be under his constant supervision. Fortunately it opened its doors a year before his death, enabling him to see the accomplishment of his life-long ambition—an institution of higher learning.

The grounds of the university are said to be the most beautiful of any campus in the United States. The architecture is in complete harmony with the surroundings and the famous serpentine wall, one brick in thickness, is still a marvel to all architects.

Which President Is This?

Made his own edition of the Bible.
Gave us our system of dimes and dollars.
Founded a state university at 82.
Retired $20,000 in debt.
Died on the 4th of July.
Almost went bankrupt entertaining his friends.
Worked 32 years in building a 33-room house.
An inventor.
Sold his private library to Congress for $24,000.
America's first great architect.

(See page 10.)

Jefferson watched the work of construction on the buildings, driving down each day from Monticello, to superintend the work. When the weather was too severe for a personal visit, or he was physically unable to ride, he observed the workmen through a long telescope from his porch.

He enjoyed entertaining the young students at his own table in Monticello, and talked with them personally regarding their problems. Monticello was built for himself, but the University of Virginia was a labor of love for others.

An Exhausted President

Jackson was a constant sufferer during his last years as president. He had an irritating cough and repeated hemorrhage from the lungs, caused by a bullet wound received in a duel many years before. When his second term ended, he remained two weeks in the White House as a guest of his successor, Van Buren, because he was too exhausted to start the long trip home over the rough roads in his carriage.

What President was 25 Years in Retirement and Never Revisited Washington?

John Adams, second President, was greatly embittered when defeated for re-election by his old rival, Jefferson. Rather than ride with his successor in the inaugural parade, Adams left Washington at daybreak, on horseback, for his far-off home near Boston, and never returned.

FINANCE

What President Had to Borrow Money to Attend His Own Inauguration?

Tyler was the successor to William Henry Harrison. Harrison went into office March 4, 1841, and died one month later.

Tyler, the Vice-President, lived in Williamsburg, Virginia. The messenger carrying to him the tidings of the sudden death of Harrison, traveled by boat and buggy, and on arrival found Tyler down on one knee playing marbles with his sons in the back yard. He gave Tyler the surprising news that he was now the President of the United States, and should go at once to Washington to be sworn in.

Tyler, who was always hard-pressed financially, had not yet received his first month's salary as Vice-President, and did not have sufficient funds to pay his way to Washington for his own inauguration. But willing friends loaned him the money, and he started on his eventful journey.

Lincoln Died a Wealthy Man.

Most people think that *Lincoln* died in comparative poverty, but, for his time, he was actually a wealthy man. When he became President he had notes due him amounting to $9,337.90 in a bank in Springfield, Illinois.

In the spring of 1864, a year before his death, he walked into the Treasury office at Washington and laid down sixty-eight thousand dollars in treasury notes, demand notes and other securities, which he desired converted into bonds. Most of this money had been saved from his presidential salary.

When Lincoln died he left four uncashed salary checks, amounting to $7,921.23 and a deposit of $17,-098.64, in one of the banks in Springfield, Illinois. At the final administration of his $110,974.62 estate, three years after his death, his wife and two sons shared equally.

A Bankrupt President

When *Jefferson* was married he and his wife owned together 5900 acres of land and 185 slaves. Yet, when he died 54 years later, after a lifetime of service for his country, his estate was practically insolvent.

When Was a $10,000 Gift Presented to a President's Wife?

Both *President Taft* and his wife were very popular in Washington. They made many friends. When they retired from the White House sixty society ladies of Washington raised a fund of $10,000 for a present for Mrs. Taft. It was a beautiful diamond necklace and was presented as a token of their esteem. Mr. Taft also received a pearl scarf pin. Social life under their regime was at its height.

The state dinners cost from $8.00 to $12.00 per plate. One diplomatic dinner cost around $1200.

The President's wife had splendid taste in music and invited many young artists to give performances in the White House, thus aiding them in their professional career. She was a splendid pianist and often played in the evening when they were alone in the family circle.

Mrs. Taft personally examined and approved all White House bills; always she had been a careful manager and a great help to her husband. Her fortune, while not large, aided materially in the family expense. She was practical, capable, and had a wonderful memory for names and faces. She visited many countries and was noted for her skill as a linguist. She was a constant student of political affairs.

When Taft retired from the presidency, he stepped to the pulpit of the All-Souls Unitarian Church, in Washington, and bade farewell to the entire congregation.

Sixteen Years to Pay a Grocer's Bill

Lincoln began his practice of law in Springfield. He worked sixteen years to pay a wholesale grocer's bill which he had contracted while in the grocery business at New Salem, Illinois—"Honest Abe."

What President Was Charged with Eating with a Gold Spoon?

In 1837, the widower, *Van Buren* and his four sons moved into the White House. A neat man, of polished manner and luxurious tastes, he was irked at the condition in which he found the White House.

Immediately after inauguration he instituted changes with the aid of an appropriation of $27,000 which was made for that purpose.

Much of the worn furniture was replaced, the draperies and hangings cleaned, quantities of expensive cut glass and china were imported, and the whole building modernized. The White House took on an entirely different aspect from that of the administration of Jackson. In fact, an aspect of elegance filled the mansion. But all did not accept the innovations with pleasure. A billiard table both disgusted and amazed the Whigs who thereafter became relentless in their criticism. It was they who said the President ate with a golden spoon. His magnificent coach taunted them, and his elaborate household, with an imported chef, caused the back woodsmen visiting Washington to take home with them tales of pomp and extravagance. Although elaborate dinners increased, the number of guests decreased to a few select friends, and the number of public receptions was cut to one each year, and was without refreshments. Such practices caused widespread indignation and laid the foundation for the Whig victory in 1840.

Who Was the Only President to Pay Off the National Debt?

Jackson greatly disliked the National Bank, vetoed the bill to recharter it, and withdrew the Government funds from its keeping. In 1836 he used these monies to pay off the National debt, and even divided a surplus among the states. However, this had a bad effect as the sudden withdrawal of funds caused the panic of 1837 under Jackson's successor, Van Buren.

What President Sold His Private Library to Congress for $24,000?

Jefferson was very proud of his library. It was the result of almost fifty years of collecting, and covered a wide variety of subjects. He had spared no expense in its accumulation. Many of the priceless volumes were procured in France while he was minister there, and others were the gifts of Franklin and of other noted men.

When the Library of Congress was burned by the British, in 1814, Jefferson made it known that he was willing to sell his private library to the Government. The offer was accepted and the sum of $23,950

Who Is This?

Never drew his salary until retirement.
Lived and died in a village of six hundred
   people.
Charged with eating with a gold spoon.
Many newspapers of the country made no
   mention of his death.
Five thousand dollars offered for scenic wall-
   paper from his old home.

(See page 10.)

was paid for 6487 volumes. They were hauled over the mountains in twelve wagons to Washington. Many of the more valuable volumes, bearing Jefferson's private mark of ownership, are carefully preserved in the rare book department of the Library of Congress.

What Is Franklin D. Roosevelt's Wealth?

Franklin D. Roosevelt has never known financial embarrassment, for in addition to salaries derived from public offices, he has inherited money from several sources. He was bequeathed $100,000 from his father, and a similar amount from a step-brother. His mother's wealth is estimated at $700,000, and his wife's private income is $7,500 a year.

Hyde Park, the beautiful 600-acre estate overlooking the Hudson, near Poughkeepsie, New York, is owned by his mother. He has made it his home for years.

What President Received More Money for His Autobiography Than He Had Earned in a Lifetime?

Grant's life ended with tragedy and despair. The General had found himself bankrupt, in 1884, after the failure of his lone business enterprise, for he had shouldered all responsibility and endeavored to compensate each one who had lost his savings through confidence in him.

Mark Twain approached Grant, offering splendid royalties for his memoirs, and Grant cheerfully accepted, hoping that through this source he might pay his debts and provide for his family. The ex-president had never prided himself on literary style, but he was informed that his direct way of telling

4584

interesting anecdotes of his military experiences would suffice. So the last few months of his life he spent writing his memoirs.

Work progressed nicely until he became increasingly conscious of a sharp pain which had suddenly developed in his mouth. He had thought it would soon disappear, but as it grew worse, he sought medical advice. An examination disclosed cancer and no hope could be given for his recovery.

Hence Grant's writing became a race with death. He was soon forced to abandon dictation because of his throat and thereafter continued in longhand. He clung desperately to his task, often finding it necessary to rest for long intervals because of pain and exhaustion. The last chapter was completed but a week before his death.

Needless to say, Grant never lived to see the printed books. But the American public was anxious to buy them, and Mrs. Grant received in royalties almost half a million dollars—more than her husband had earned in his lifetime.

What President Became a Bankrupt Three Years Before His Election?

McKinley served in Congress for fourteen years, and became one of the best known statesmen in the United States; yet, he was defeated for re-election in 1890. A short time later he was held responsible for notes which he had endorsed for a friend in Youngstown, Ohio. Their payment took his entire personal savings as well as the $100,000 fortune of Mrs. McKinley. In addition, Mark Hanna raised another $100,000 among McKinley's many friends in order to fully pay the obligations. Three years later, in 1896, this man who had faced his creditors and had mortgaged his entire future was elected president.

What President, While in Office, Paid $3,000 a Year for a Private Home?

When the National Government was moved from New York to Philadelphia, a beautiful home was offered *Washington,* at national expense. He said, however, that he would not live in a home unless he either owned it or rented it privately. He finally rented a brick house from Robert Morris for which he paid an annual rental of $3,000. Washington remodeled the private dwelling and enlarged the stables to accommodate twelve horses.

Washington accepted no salary for his services as president.

A President Who Loved to Travel

Taft was the first president to have the new salary of $75,000 per year, instead of $50,000. He also had an additional $25,000 for traveling expenses. He traveled 150,000 miles in four years.

What President Was Once a Multimillionaire?

Hoover was a very successful mining engineer, both from a professional and financial standpoint. He was our most widely traveled president, and was as well-known in Europe as in America. Orphaned when a small boy, he worked his way through Leland Stanford University by conducting a laundry agency.

Upon graduation Hoover wielded pick and shovel in western mines, and at 22 was earning $7,500 a year. Soon he caught the attention of English capitalists for whom he managed lead, copper and silver mines in China and Australia. When 34 he had offices in London, New York, and San Francisco. But his greatest financial gains were from the rich mines of Burma, where he had many profitable holdings.

At the opening of the World War in 1914, when only forty years of age, Hoover's estimated wealth was four million dollars. Like other Americans, however, he lost heavily during the depression. In 1932, while President, his estimated wealth was reduced to three-quarters of a million dollars, carefully invested in the best of securities. Hoover was always known for his philanthropic gifts.

When Did 50 Congressmen Devote Their Entire Savings to the Election of a President?

The first election of *Jackson* was very cleverly handled by Van Buren who brought him forth as a man of the people. Jackson was persuaded to resign from the Senate, where he might have made some enemies, and retire to his farm, in Tennessee, while the country was still flooded with accounts of his military exploits and social qualities. So far-reaching was the campaign that more than fifty congressmen expended and pledged all they were worth in setting up printing presses to forward Jackson's campaign.

What President Never Accepted Gifts?

Presidents, through all the years, have been embarrassed by the great number of gifts showered upon them. *Buchanan* made it a rule, which other presidents before his time had neglected, never to accept presents of any value, not even from his most intimate friends or political supporters. Thus it became a part of the duties of his secretary, Mr. Henry, to immediately return any gifts with the thanks of the President.

Buchanan's salary of $25,000 per year did not defray the actual household expenses of the White House, so he found it necessary to draw liberally upon his private means for his expenses and generous charities.

Guess Who

Was our only bachelor President.
Paid $800 for a set of harness.
Never accepted gifts.
His niece was his housekeeper.
Only President from Pennsylvania.

(See page 10.)

DEATHS

Which Three Presidents Died on the 4th of July?

Adams and *Jefferson* had been associated for many years. On July 4, 1776, they completed the Declaration of Independence. Jefferson was its author; Adams its defender. Later, in Washington's Cabinet Adams was vice-president, and Jefferson secretary of state. Adams, coming up for re-election as president, was defeated by Jefferson, and their friendship ceased for several years. However, through the efforts of a mutual friend, they carried on a very interesting correspondence with each other in later years.

July 4, 1826, drew near. It was the fiftieth anniversary of the Declaration of Independence, and both Jefferson and Adams were still living. Promient statesmen thought it would be appropriate for these two grand old men to be together on that day. But Jefferson, at his home in Monticello, Virginia, was extremely feeble; and Adams in Braintree, Massachusetts, near Boston, was at the point of death.

July 4th dawned. John Adams lost consciousness in the early morning hours. He was awakened by the sounds of cannon celebrating the occasion. He rallied, and a friend at his bedside asked him if he knew what day it was. Pondering a moment he said, "Yes, it's the glorious 4th." Then remembering the fifty intervening years, his face grew bright and his last words were, "But my old friend Thomas Jefferson still survives." However, he was wrong, for Jefferson had died but two hours previously. It seems strange indeed, that these two grand old patriots who had labored together so many years in their country's cause, should die on the fiftieth anniversary of the Declaration of Independence.

The third president to die on the 4th of July was *Monroe,* aged 81. This was in 1831.

Thus of the first five presidents of the United States, three of them died on the 4th of July.

What President's Body Lay in State in Fourteen Different Cities?

Lincoln died on Saturday, April 15th, but the White House funeral services were not held until six days later. At the foot of the President's casket in the funeral car was placed a small casket, containing the body of his son, Willie Lincoln, who died of smallpox three years before.

The journey to Springfield, Illinois, covered practically the same cities as had been traveled by Lincoln on his trip to Washington, more than four years before. Three men who had also been with the President, on the first trip, accompanied the funeral train.

On Tuesday, April 25, the body lay in state in the New York City Hall, and the casket was left open all night. The crowds at night were even greater than those in the day time, filling the side streets around the square in every direction. Torches and gas street lights were used for illumination. A German chorus of seventy voices began to sing shortly after midnight. When the body was removed to the depot, a huge funeral procession was formed, every organization, both civil and military, being represented. The procession took four hours to pass.

At the end of the parade was a company of 200 Negroes, recently freed from slavery. They had appealed to the Secretary of War for permission to march, which was finally granted. The colored men were preceded by a squadron of police, and another squadron of officers followed. It was feared that their presence in the parade might cause a riot, but there was no disturbance. Several white men walked with them and many people applauded as they passed.

All along the route, whether day or night, the funeral train was greeted at cities, villages and country cross-roads by large crowds. In every town the bells tolled as the train passed, and minute-guns were fired. The stations were draped in black, and at many points arches were erected over the tracks. Crepe, evergreens and flags were used on the bridges. Notices of the exact time of arrival had been given in advance.

The body lay in state at Baltimore, Harrisburg, Philadelphia, New York City, Albany, Syracuse, Rochester, Buffalo, Cleveland, Columbus, Indianapolis, Chicago and Springfield.

Neighbors and friends at the various farm houses gathered to see the funeral train. Large bonfires were built at night, around which the citizens of the countryside gathered to pay their last respects to their beloved president. Much of the journey of the famous funeral train was made in the rain, but this did not prevent the patient crowds from waiting.

On Monday, May 1, the train reached Chicago. The body was taken to the court house, where an endless stream of citizens passed by. The journey to Springfield was made at night. The whole population of the country lined the route. The train arrived at 9:00 A. M., and the body lay in state for twenty-four hours.

By the time it had reached Springfield, the face of Lincoln was black and shrunken, as he had died eighteen days before. The body was laid to rest in Oak Ridge Cemetery, in a tomb, with his little son, Willie, by his side.

What President, While in Office, Died from Exposure to Heat?

On July 4, 1850, *Taylor* assisted in laying the corner stone of Washington's Monument. The day was extremely hot and the speaker's stand had no protection from the sun. The services were long, and General Taylor was overcome by the intense heat. At their conclusion he rode to the White House, drank a quantity of cold milk and ate fresh cherries. His death five days later was attributed to cholera morbus. He served but one-third of his term, being the second Whig president to die in office.

A Sad Death

Dr. Rixey, his private physician, said that *McKinley's* bullet-wound was not necessarily fatal, but that death occurred because he lacked proper physical resistance. Instead of taking regular exercise, McKinley, while President, would sit for hours and read to his invalid wife. He lingered six days after being shot, but lacked the physical reserve and strength to meet the emergency. Mrs. McKinley never returned to the White House after the assassination at Buffalo. She outlived her husband six years.

What Caused Harding's Death?

Senator Watson, of Indiana, called on Harding the day before he started on his Alaskan trip. He put his hand on the President's shoulder and said, "Warren, I am telling you good-bye, and I think for the last time. I know about the condition of your heart, and your general state of health, and I do not believe that you will ever survive this trip."

Harding must have had a premonition that he might not return, because he made his will, changed some of his investments, sold some property, and thoroughly put his house in order.

His vitality had been weakened by a bad case of the "flu" a short time previously, and he complained to a near relative of an exhausted condition. He had an enlarged heart, hardening of the arteries, and a tendency toward diabetes. Even before his presidency he had been a patient, on several occasions, at the Battle Creek Sanitarium.

Harding delivered 85 addresses in six weeks, visited fifty-four cities in the United States and Alaska, and made as many as eleven speeches a day. His duties were various and many, extending from the driving of a binder in a Kansas wheat field, to the driving of a gold railroad spike in frozen Alaska.

The strenuous activities of continued travel, the great physical exhaustion, changes of altitude, and the constant strain were too much for a man with an enlarged and weakened heart. He presented medals to Boy Scouts and dedicated public buildings. He addressed crowds of people as late as midnight, and as early as 6:30 in the morning, speaking on a variety of subjects. His rest was continually broken. Everyone was waiting to see the President and hear him speak.

Even between cities Harding got but little rest, being accompanied by governors and congressmen who were anxious to convey to the President their own local problems. He never shirked a responsibility, giving his last ounce of strength to the people who longed to hear him speak. His schedule had been carefully planned, with allowances for everything but rest.

On his way south from Alaska, at Seattle, there was a suggestion of collapse. Those nearest him saw it, but he rallied and finished the address.

Do You Know Him?

Never voted until he was 62 years old.
His wife smoked a corn-cob pipe in the White
House.
Died from exposure to heat.
Had his horse pastured on White House lawn.
His daughter eloped with Jefferson Davis.

(See page 10.)

Dr. Wilbur, President of Stanford University, was one of the five physicians who took care of Harding in his last illness at San Francisco. He wrote an article concerning it, two months later, for the *Saturday Evening Post*.

The primary cause of his illness was pneumonia, followed by a cerebral hemorrhage which caused instant death.

A Son Dies

A year after *Lincoln* took office, his young son, Willie, succumbed to smallpox. He was a great favorite with everyone in the White House, and was seen with his father many times. Mrs. Lincoln was so overcome with grief that she never again entered the Green Room where the body of the child had lain in state. Willie was buried in Washington, but the small casket was removed when Lincoln's body was sent to Springfield, Illinois.

Where Was Lincoln's Bodyguard When He Was Shot?

Late on the afternoon of April 14, Colonel Crook, his private bodyguard, accompanied Lincoln to the offices of the War Department. The President was much depressed and his step was unusually slow. He seemed to have a premonition of danger. Lincoln said, "Crook, do you know, I believe that there are men who want to take my life, and I have no doubt they will do it." He spoke with much conviction and told Crook that he had absolute confidence in each of his bodyguards. Later, he intimated that he intended to go to the theatre that evening with Mrs. Lincoln.

When his bodyguard turned to leave, at the White House steps, Lincoln said, "Good-bye, Crook." Previously his parting salute had always been, "Good-night, Crook."

John Parker, another secret service man, took Mr. Crook's place at the supper hour and accompanied Lincoln to the theatre. It was always the custom for the guard to sit at the rear of the box in the passage way and protect the president. Parker confessed to Mr. Crook that instead of staying there and guarding Lincoln, he went to the front of the balcony where he could see the play and took a seat there. The door of the President's box was closed and Lincoln never knew that the guard had left his post of duty. Mr. Buckingham, the doorkeeper, stated that Booth went in and out of the theatre five times before he shot the President, each time stimulating himself with whiskey. Each time he carefully surveyed the theatre, and evidently saw that the guard was not at his post.

Parker knew that he had failed in his duty and looked like a convicted criminal the next day. He was never the same man afterwards. Strange to say, the authorities never investigated the matter, and Colonel Crook did not make it known until after Parker's death.

What President's Funeral Has Never Been Paid For?

Garfield had three funerals: One at Elberon, New Jersey, where he died; another in Washington, where the body lay in state for three days; and a third at Cleveland, where he was buried.

The funeral director in Washington, employed by the Government, was W. R. Speare. According to the itemized statement in the *Congressional Record,* he furnished a total of 93 carriages, 118 white sashes, 12 black sashes, 30 pairs of white kid gloves, 14 pairs of black kid gloves, a hearse with 6 white horses and groom attendants. It was perhaps the greatest funeral Washington had ever seen.

Mr. Speare presented his bill of $1,890.50 to the Government repeatedly. Fifty-five thousand dollars had been voted by Congress for the care of Garfield, after the assassination, but the undertaker, who did his work so faithfully, never received a penny.

A Cruel Assassin

Guitteau who assassinated *Garfield* admitted, after his capture, that he had trailed the president for more than six weeks. That on a previous occasion he had an opportunity to kill him while standing in the depot, but that Mrs. Garfield clung to his arm so tenderly and looked so frail, that he did not have the heart to fire the fatal shot. Mrs. Garfield outlived her husband 37 years.

How Many Presidents Died in the White House?

Six presidents died during their terms of office. Three were assassinated and three died of natural causes. Of the six, however, only two died in the White House, William Henry Harrison and Zachary Taylor.

Lincoln, although assassinated in Washington, died in a small actors' boarding house across the street from the theatre, in a bed which had once been occupied by John Wilkes Booth, his assassin.

Garfield was assassinated in the railway station in Washington, but survived for more than two months, finally being taken to Elberon, New Jersey, where he died.

McKinley was shot in Buffalo, while visiting the Pan-American Exposition, and died there six days later. Harding died in San Francisco, after three days illness.

An Imposing Funeral

William H. Harrison was the first president to die in office. The funeral was more imposing and better arranged than his inauguration. There were twenty-six pall-bearers and a procession composed of 10,000 people which extended more than two miles.

Respect for a Predecessor

Arthur wore mourning for his assassinated predecessor Garfield for six months. He declined all invitations to theatrical performances and gave no state entertainments at the White House during that time.

What President Took Out a $25,000 Life Insurance Policy Two Months Before His Assassination?

Garfield was insured by the New York Life Insurance Company. He did not pay cash for the policy, but gave his note for $1,415.44. His widow collected the insurance after his death and paid the note.

This original cancelled note is now on file in the probate judge's office at Painesville, Ohio, where Garfield's estate was settled.

Slow Communication

Although *Washington* died at his home in Mt. Vernon on December 14, 1799, it was not until five days later that the news reached Congress in Philadelphia, then the seat of Government.

Is an Ill-Fated President Elected Every Twenty Years?

For almost a century the presidents who met ill-fate were elected every twenty years.

William H. Harrison—1840, died in a month.

Abraham Lincoln—1860, assassinated.

James A. Garfield—1880, assassinated.

William McKinley—1900, assassinated.

Warren G. Harding—1920, untimely death.

Arlington Cemetery

Taft is the only president to be buried in Arlington Cemetery in Washington.

Madison lived, died and was buried on the same farm in Virginia.

Bachelor President

Nearly all of the presidents are buried with their families. Buchanan remained a bachelor his entire life and is buried alone in the cemetery at Lancaster, Pennsylvania.

What President, While in Office, Died from Exposure to Cold?

William Henry Harrison was inaugurated at 68 years of age. He was a veteran of many military campaigns and was inaugurated the first Whig president, just 30 years after his great victory over the Indians at Tippecanoe.

March 4, 1841, was perhaps one of the coldest inaugural days in history. Friends from Baltimore had provided a splendid carriage, drawn by four white horses, for the president's use in the parade. He said, however, that he would rather ride a horse and, in spite of the entreaties of his friends, rode without an overcoat.

Who Is This?

Was also a preacher.
Took out a $25,000 life insurance policy four
  months before his death.
His funeral has never been paid for.
Was once a college president.

(See page 10.)

He carried his hat in his hand along most of the route, bowing to the fifty thousand spectators who lined the sidewalks of Pennsylvania Avenue. The procession moved slowly and finally arrived at the Capitol, where President Harrison, without hat or overcoat, delivered his inaugural address in the face of a cold northeast wind.

It lasted an hour and a quarter. The exposure was too much. Pneumonia developed, and harrassed by countless office seekers, who worried him day and night, this 68-year-old president died after one month in office. His wife never reached the White House because of illness, yet she outlived her husband by a quarter of a century.

What President's Body Was Removed from the Tomb in an Attempted Robbery?

In 1876 two counterfeiters in Chicago greatly desired to obtain the release of a partner from the penitentiary. They conceived the idea that if they could steal *Lincoln's* body from his tomb, and hide it in the sand dunes of Indiana, they might bargain for the freedom of their partner in exchange for the body. Unknowingly they took into their confidence a Pinkerton detective who pretended to be an expert grave robber and who readily agreed to join in the adventure.

The three left Chicago by train for Springfield. However, on the same train were other officers who stayed in the sleeping car, got off at the railroad yards, went immediately to the Lincoln tomb, and there secreted themselves. Upon arriving in Springfield one of the robbers was to get the tools, another to study the lay of the land, and the detective to get a horse and wagon. The Pinkerton man had planned to work on the outside, and when the casket was ready for removal, to light a cigar at which signal the officers would rush upon the criminals and arrest them.

At the last moment, the counterfeiters changed their plans, deciding that the detective should stay inside the tomb and hold the "dark lantern" so that the other two might work. As a result, the detective could not slip out and give the appointed signal.

When the casket was ready for removal and partly out of the window, the counterfeiters told the detective to get his horse and wagon. This he pretended to do, but instead gave the belated signal.

The officers rushed around the tomb, found the casket ready for removal, but no grave robbers. They had been resting under nearby bushes after their exhausting labors and quickly fled in the excitement.

However, their haunts were known, and they were arrested in Chicago a few days later. Of course, the thieves were brought to trial, but the singular situation was that at that time the State of Illinois had no law concerning grave robbery. The worst penalty that could be inflicted was a year's imprisonment for the breaking of a lock.

The thieves served their sentences and then quietly returned to civil life, one of them practicing as a veterinary in an Illinois town.

Which President?

Only Speaker of the House to become President.

Twice defeated for Governor of his own State.

His wife was his private secretary.

Died from overwork four months after retirement.

Survived by his wife forty-six years.

(See page 10.)

INDEX